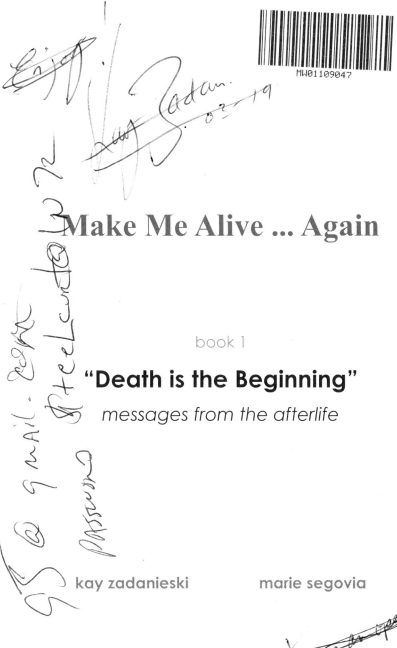

Make Me Alive ... Again

book 1

"Death is the Beginning"

messages from the afterlife

kay zadanieski   marie segovia

Make Me Alive Again
Death is the Beginning
Non-fiction. Copyright © 2013 by Kay Zadanieski.

Library of Congress Catalog Number: 2013939250

For information, contact
Inspire Publications Inc

via email to

info@inspirepublications.com

or in writing to

2 North Cascade, Suite 1100,
Colorado Springs, CO 80903

ISBN-10: 0988911515
ISBN-13: 978-0-9889115-1-2

Cover design by Nick Zelinger

To my beloved Husband.
You are truly amazing in your love and support.
In that you have been with me throughout all of this
is a testament to the wonderful man you are.

To my Co-Author, friend and confidante.
Without you this book would never have been written.

To my dearest "Cat."
As we walk together along this rocky path of existence, perhaps we
may stumble, but we always catch
each other, steady each other, and continue our
journey onward.

Brother,
I hope you read
this book!
o

We Love You
Always Your Only
BaBy Sister
Lyndsey Sutherland x

Christmas
2023

contents

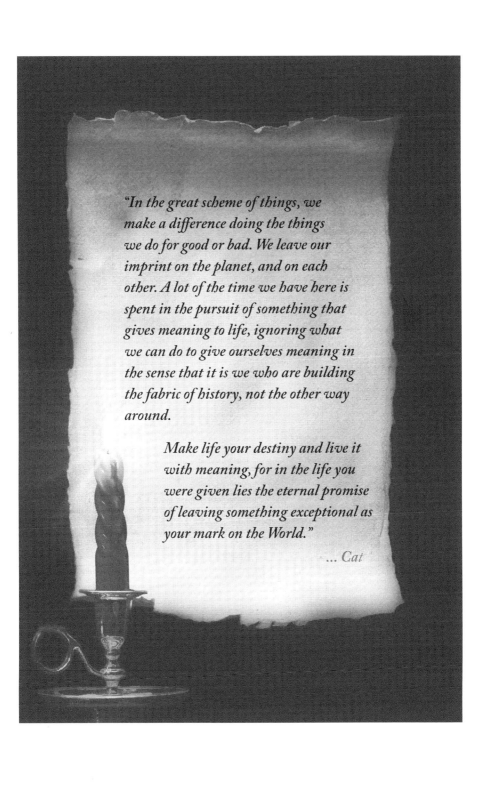

"In the great scheme of things, we make a difference doing the things we do for good or bad. We leave our imprint on the planet, and on each other. A lot of the time we have here is spent in the pursuit of something that gives meaning to life, ignoring what we can do to give ourselves meaning in the sense that it is we who are building the fabric of history, not the other way around.

Make life your destiny and live it with meaning, for in the life you were given lies the eternal promise of leaving something exceptional as your mark on the World."

... Cat

foreword

... *Cat*

I **had nothing to lose.**

It's not easy to explain, but there I was – in a strange place, trying to remember where I had seen her previously. She seemed familiar, yet a stranger and I could not stop watching her as she went about her life.

My life had ended and I had nowhere to be, although I had everything I had ever been in my most recent memories. I had just had to leave – I didn't want to. My body was cancer-ridden. I couldn't do anything other than listen and talk a little about things loved to people I loved.

I know now that I was dying, but then I knew it too. Dying is an odd reality – it is the most external, yet the most personal and introspective experience I could ever have imagined. Just as I had thought I was invincible, I was faced with reality. It hit me hard. I had fucked up so badly. My life became my conscience and my life became all I was able to see.

I am not the worthy one in the respect of being given better chances than most, but I can say that I had that opportunity, and I took it. I knew, feeling as I did afterwards, that I had done all I could do, save a miracle. I looked for it.

I didn't find it. I knew I had nothing left. It was a life-ending situation. Just as I thought. It happened. I died.

I woke up. I woke up in my bed in that late afternoon in ******. The light was such that I could not tell if it were early morning or evening. I remember the trees casting shadows and so I knew it was the latter. I got up. I felt better. It was not my usual bedroom, as I could no longer manage stairs. It was the bedroom I shared with my wife, the bedroom that was mine before I was sick – the bedroom of our marriage.

It was so blissful to wake up to her scent. It was everything I had needed for so long. Her scent was the most beautiful I had ever known. Her hair was so full of it. Her warm hands in mine, her beautiful face I will never forget as she gave birth to our children. Her love, her doing, her wanting me. My wanting her.

I had lost her. I know that I did. She was distant. I couldn't be her lover any more. I didn't wish to be in this state. I couldn't find a way out. I had lost everything – my business particularly. Everything I had worked for wasn't mine now, it was someone else's and I felt useless – about as useless as a lemon in a cake made from candy. It was the end. I knew it.

So, why I didn't know it when I woke up, I'm not sure. I'm not sure I could envisage being dead. I felt great, so I went downstairs. They were all in the kitchen. I heard them. They were talking about me as though I wasn't there and no one looked up at me. I was dreaming, I supposed.

I ate a little fruit and went to my usual room to watch TV. The bed was not made. The linens were gone and my glasses were not where I'd left them. Okay, I have another pair in my office. I'm trying to put the TV on but the remote must be out of battery. Too bad – I'm tired anyway. I go back upstairs and get back into bed, sleepy and feeling good listening to the cars coming down the street at the side of the house.

She's there in the morning, when I wake up. All soft and warm like the pretty, lovely woman I married all those years ago. I reach for her. She doesn't wake. I'm at my best in the morning. I want her before I go to work, before the kids get up. Oh, work! I can't wait. I know I can be there again, but for now, I just want her. Her sleep goes on. I can't wake her and I'm not going to try. She's obviously really tired.

I get dressed and try to make a couple of calls from the system in my office. It's not working. I email instead. It won't send, for fuck's sake. Why won't anything work? I'm not happy. I'm going to go to the office. I no more think it, than I'm there. Okay. Dreaming.

I walk toward my old office, past the conference room, looking for ******. I hear voices. They're talking about me. I have to listen, I suppose, if I hear my name – I'm not one to mind my own business around here! I hear them talking about me in the past tense but then I haven't been here in weeks. I've forgotten that. Just who is going to see me first, and welcome me back, I'm wondering, just as the door opens and ****** comes out, walking right toward me and then, right past me as if I don't exist. I call after him. Nothing. I stand alone in the hallway. I'm not dreaming; I just know it. It's something more, I know and I don't want to face it. I died, didn't I?

I go to my office. My furniture is still there. I sit and try to remember something that happened before yesterday. When did I fall asleep? I can recall them all in my room. Did my ****** make it? I'd called her. I feel I knew. My God, I knew I couldn't hang on when I had nothing left, physically. It was all in the cards, and I'm not what you would call a lucky one that pulled an Ace this time. I had to face it.

I remember that I felt suddenly pain-free and a little light-headed, like I do when I get that pre-anesthesia shot, that nice warm drifty feeling and it's like nothing matters. I was so tired, I couldn't talk any more, just look at my kids. I wanted to tell them why. I wanted to be able to tell them so many things but I couldn't.

I just …

K … Cat. Are you okay?

C ... *I'm trying to – but it's so hard.*

K ... Do you need a minute?

C ... *No. I'm okay.*

I just looked at them and at my beautiful wife. She looked so tired. She was trying to smile and hold it together.

I'm not sure I remember anything past that. I felt so very tired. It was a trying to hold onto a present that I couldn't hold onto, and so I let it go. It's strange, but perhaps that's when I saw her – her standing there, with her hand stretched out to me. I didn't know her Being. She was sort of like a ghost in the background, waiting. I'm not sure. I'm just trying to remember that bracing fall into another place. It was as though I traveled on to somewhere I didn't want to and I couldn't stop. I'm not about to say into a light – there wasn't a light. I felt lost in space, like it wanted me but I didn't want it, in a place I didn't want to be. I wanted to be with my family. I didn't know what I was supposed to do. I guess that's when I woke up in my bed.

Having this in mind, I'm still not sure I'm not dreaming. I'm not sure of anything just now. Just how did I get here? I am now at the very edge of the Universe. I'm not going to step off. I can't. I'm staying here, just right here in this room. I have to. I can't leave just like that. I'm afraid I'll never find the way back if I leave.

I go to the window and I see flowers on the lawn outside my little office, like a great wave of color, and beyond them the street and more flowers, but these are being placed there. Why are so many people leaving flowers there? I go to take a look. "******", "Rest in Peace," one note reads. Oh God, it's true. Fuck. I'm dead. I'm not dreaming. Fuck. I'm trapped in a nightmare. I'm dead. My legs give way. I'm on the sidewalk. I'm crying like a baby; I'm screaming a primal scream inside my head. I'm so absolutely terrified. I don't want to be dead. Fuck, I'm still here. I'm still *****, and I'm still here. I can't be dead, it's impossible.

Just then, I see ***** cross the hallway. I'm sitting there on the bench I used to sit on to pull on sneakers. I'm able to see her but she can't see me, can she? I *know she can't. I look at the floor. There's a little spider web on the end of the bench and as I gently tap it, the architect runs out from behind a leaf that had fallen there from a shoe, I suppose. I'm so focused on the little creature that it takes me a moment to realize it.*

I'm able to touch things and get a reaction.

I touch the spider, and it runs back under its leaf. I gently move the leaf and poke my new friend. She (or he) runs across the floor away from me, going toward the kitchen. I follow her slowly and poke her some more, crying tears of happiness at this small contact with another living thing. I let her alone now and go to find ******; can she feel me too? I tap her on the shoulder. Nothing. I try again, harder – still no response. I'm unable to ever hold her and she feel my love ever again. I can't bear it. She's not mine any more. My life with her is over.

Hearing our son come down the stairs, I go to him and touch him too, but the same. I can't be felt. All I have is a spider.

I'm filled with a new fear. How do I live now? I can't talk or touch. I can only listen. It's a living death. How long will it last? Forever?

I can't take it. I go for a walk around the neighborhood. I love to do that when I need to think. It's calming and just liberating to get the feel of the pavement under my feet. I'll think better now. Okay. I'm dead. I shouldn't be here. I'm still me though, just like I was before I got cancer. Getting that was like being in suspended animation some days, and I'll memorize those feelings and then put them away. I don't want to think about it now.

I'm tired. I go to sleep on the unmade bed in my room. I'm not able to rest. I have too much on my mind. I can't sleep more than an hour or two and I'm cold. I go to find a blanket. It doesn't respond when I pull at it. I just feel so useless. I can move a spider, but not my family. I can't even get a blanket.

Being so miserable, I go to ******. I know there's plenty there to amuse myself with. I just think of it, and I'm there - so cool! OK. What's everyone up to on ******? I start looking. Fuck. It's a crap deal. I mean, it's a fucking load of shit.

I left this is good hands. Now look. It's indescribable. I knew I should have made sure it was in line with my vision instead of leaving it to a bunch of shitheads. God. I'm so mad that it's just as well my body isn't capable of going insane along with it.

I'm so tired I have to rest. I know there's a room with a big couch that some of my software guys sleep on sometimes. I can go there - and I am there. It's warm from the lab equipment - a lot of mechanical energy generated by computers. I'm so sleepy and the soft hum of the hardware lulls me into a dreamless sleep.

I don't wake until I hear voices. It's eight, or maybe earlier. I know I'm about to get a glimpse of my team. I'm at the zenith of my patience. I can't tell them - I'm dead, for God's sake. I'm going home.

What I walk into throws me. ******, and my family, ******'s best friend, our sisters - the whole gang dressed in black. I don't want to know I'm really dead. It's too much. I need to go somewhere safe. I'm so frightened. What happens to me? What about my body? I know where it is. I am now certain of the fact that I am gone and I recall the Plan B. It (my body, that is) has been taken to the place I had decided upon if I didn't make it. I don't want to see it. I am still alive, it is not. It is rigid and cold in a box and I am warm and very not dead. I can't go with them to say goodbye to it. I am here, not there.

It was really a good body for a good part of my life. Tall and slim, not very muscular but I looked good. How it wasted away I can't see, although I know. It disintegrated into a useless shell and I had to leave it. I couldn't fix it. I am now without its disease and I am okay without it. It has to be put in the ground now, but still I can't watch.

I am so alone and so afraid. I don't know what to do. They leave. I follow, despite myself. I follow them to that place. I can't go in. I know what lies inside. That box. Waiting to return it to the gentle earth from which it came - a cycle of all things, and an end to become the beginning again. I, however, do not go with it.

I am going to work. I arrive at my building. I go inside from the parking lot. What I hear next cuts me to the very depths of my soul. I am so hated, I am so loved; I am the deserver of my death, I am missed – I am the God, I am the Devil.

I am. It's all I still know.

I go back to my office. It was always my place to be. I lie on the floor. I can't hold back now. The tears come. I am in a fetal position, my arms around my chest as I tear myself apart. I am lost and I don't know where to go. I can't stop the tears. I am a mess, and as I cry, I feel. I feel the absolute truth. I am dead. Game over. I'm dead.

I am becoming so tired. My tears are exhausted. I heave my chest in and out with dry aggression, my Being coming back, my heart beating. I have to Be. I collapse in a mêlée of fear and fight. The tears come once more but more quiet now, as I have no more energy to cry them. I am in the worst of situations.

As I am lying there, I begin to feel energy apart from mine. What it is I don't know, but it's touching me. I am being gently pulled by it and I'm afraid again. I didn't want the last one and I don't know that I want this one but all else is gone. I am too tired. I just let it happen.

I'm in a different place now and she's there. The one I saw. I am so afraid but so very pulled to her. I don't know her, but she is all I have and it's the newness of everything, coupled with the desire of the old, I am in now.

I have learned to live, and learned to love again.

preface
... Marie

D eath … the final mystery we all face, and the one which we understand the least. Where we come from is the easy part … it is well documented, photographed, and witnessed by numerous people. But the subject of death … where we GO …has occupied the minds of humans since the beginning of recorded history. Pyramids, cathedrals, paintings, sculptures and writings are testament to either our belief in the after-life, or our quest for answers about it. But in the final analysis, no one really knows for sure, even if they think they do.

WHY we have such a fascination with the after-life is easy enough to understand. We simply don't want to believe that all of our life experience and personal growth goes for naught at the end, and that we simply "are not" any more. Like the Peggy Lee song, "Is That All There Is?" that leaves us dangling, we want to think that there is more, that we have an eternal purpose.

We may scoff at those who talk of having been abducted by aliens, but listen with intense interest when someone describes a near death experience (NDE). We want to know what it was like … did you see a light? Did you see your family? We want to know what to expect. But can we really know? Recent reports state that the NDE actually reveals more about your culture. For instance, many Africans see it as a bad omen; Japanese report seeing rivers and beautiful flowers; East Indians say Heaven is a huge bureaucracy where they are sent back because of clerical errors; Micronesian natives relate that Heaven is a big American city with lots of noise. Religion plays a huge role, of course. Christianity is based on the assurance of life after death, as Jesus' story is related in the Bible, and Eastern religions lean toward reincarnation as the next step.

Mention a ghost, and suddenly everyone is intrigued. It comes as no surprise that Hallowe'en is one of the most popular events in the year. All Hallow's Eve, its original name, has become more important than the holy days it precedes - All Saints Day, on Nov. 1 and All Souls Day on Nov. 2. (Also called Dia de los Muertos, Day of the Dead.) This yearly reminder of death and what lies beyond serves to rekindle our passion for knowledge.

Stories of ghosts and ghostly apparitions enliven us. We flock to see films about them, we read books about them, and we visit places considered haunted to see if we might catch our own glimpse of one. While staying at the Hollywood Roosevelt Hotel, I looked in the mirror where Marilyn Monroe is supposed to be seen on occasion (no luck) and stood outside the room where Montgomery Clift is often heard practicing his trumpet (no luck again). The spirits of the Hotel Stanley in Estes Park, Colorado sparked horror-genre master Stephen King to use it as the location of "The Shining". One of my favorite films as a young girl was "The Canterbury Ghost," with Charles Laughton portraying a cowardly soul forced to haunt a castle until he perform a heroic, noble act of courage. Yes, ghosts do intrigue us, and we wonder why they stick around.

Even if you have not personally experienced the presence of one who has passed, chances are you know someone who has. My mother did, my daughter has this ability, and so does my friend, Kay. Some people, it seems, are attuned to higher energies, much as animals sense sounds and vibrations beyond those our physical capabilities allow us to perceive. The key here is ENERGY – the simple definition being the capacity of a physical system to do work. But we have learned that we are energy beings, and Physics distills this even further down to the neutrons, protons and electrons in each atom, in each molecule, in each cell of our bodies. Science also tells us that energy cannot be destroyed. Could this be the origin of our consciousness? Our soul? Is this what the so-called ghost really is?

At the Winter Solstice, Kay held a Yule Celebration dinner for a few friends. She rather casually mentioned at one point that "we have a ghost in the house." Knowing her as one who has frequently experienced such entities, our reaction was light-hearted curiosity, some questions, and quips about "another one visiting Kay!" It was not until a later date that she revealed to me the visits were continuing, and some of the particulars were quite astonishing. She also shared some of the essays she said were written by him. I realized immediately that this was NOT her writing, nor her style of speaking. This was indeed a strong entity who was questioning his very being, who railed at not being able to continue his work, and who, over time, became more understanding of his current state, although perhaps not quite so accepting of it.

As time goes on, the communication and writings continue, and each successive exchange brings yet more insight into his phase of existence … his longings, concerns, frustrations and his growth. What he has revealed has given us endless new thoughts about life after death. His description of his own death experience is filled with pain … and wonder. The encounter between Kay and "Cat" (as she has named him) has been a gift in ways too numerous to count.

From subsequent writings we can surmise that after death we do have a choice. Our energy/spirit/soul can choose to stay, go, grow, help, learn, or do whatever it deems necessary. The essays written by Cat reveal a sentient being capable of great introspection and spiritual growth.

WHO he is, is unimportant. It is WHAT he says that is too significant to be ignored.

While some of what passes between them is intensely personal, it is our belief that the revelations and reflections are so inspiring and stimulate such hopefulness that they demand to be shared with all who continue in their quest for greater understanding about that great mystery … life beyond death.

preface
... Kay

*I*t's strange how you remember exactly where you were and what you were doing when that moment in time comes along and changes your life irrevocably.

9/11/2001.
A marriage proposal.
The birth of a child.

These are the things that memories are made from. Life-changing things - either so incredibly horrific or so incredibly beautiful that they are etched into your mind forever.

What makes this pivotal event so strange is that it should not have affected me any further than a passing sympathetic thought or two toward a family who had just lost a husband, a brother, a father.

I wish I could say that I was doing something rather more interesting, but it was the simple act of cleaning the stairs leading to the lower level that became so memorable. Cat hair. The moment I learned he had passed away, I was holding a cloth full of cat hair.

I had never met him and so I digested the news and carried on with my life. It's what the living do. He was no one close and so not my place to grieve over. At least, that is the way it's supposed to be and that's just the way it was for a week or two.

It was sad. He had died.

It's not the first time I have felt the presence of the Spirit world. When I get that feeling, I know exactly what it's about. Heavy, like the air surrounding a thunderstorm, cloying, slowing me down, surrounding me in molasses. I talk to them gently and they generally leave me after a little while - perhaps just a few hours, a day perhaps. They don't know me, I don't know them. I am just an empathic energy they drifted toward.

This time, the presence is so strong that even performing the simplest of tasks seems to take all of the energy I possess. I feel so drained. It's just not moving away from me, no matter how much I try to shake it off. In fact, instead of leaving, it seems to want to attach its self more firmly. I begin to cry for no reason. Just little bouts of it at first and now I am sitting at my desk in front of the computer, my body heaving with tears, and I can't stop. These are not mine. There is no reason at all for me to cry like this. This person needs my attention, and is determined to get it.

I seldom know the names of those who visit me. Just snippets of their lives perhaps - something about how they passed over, a place. This one is not telling me. I am trying to open my mind enough for the information to come through but it really isn't. It's just clinging to me, silent.

I remember a spirit board that I have tucked away somewhere upstairs. I have never used it before but now would seem as good a time as any. So, taking the usual precautions of protecting myself and my environment before I do any kind of work with energy, I begin. Nothing. I'm patient. I sit for some time with the board, fingers gently resting on the planchette (the device that is designed to move toward the letters). My arms are beginning to grow a little weary when it starts to move, almost imperceptibly at first and then erratically as though it is searching around the board for something.

The board, I have to admit, is rather complicated. It not only has letters and numbers but a lot of words and symbols. Hell, if I were a Spirit, I would be confused too! The planchette stops for a few moments and then begins to move in a more organized fashion. I close my eyes and allow my breathing to become slow and deep, just letting it do what it wants to do. When it stops, I open my eyes.

It is spelling out a name ...

introduction
... Kay

*I*n order to follow the rules, one must first know of the existence of rules. He knows of no such thing. He is a wild and free spirit. I may know of the existence of rules set by others. I have also rather made a lifetime commitment of ignoring them.

Hence, I suppose that we were drawn to each other. One who does not recognize the accepted rules of death and one whose freedom from the barriers of both the "accepted" and the "rule," will allow him to be heard again - to speak and do as he did in the physical realm and to express himself in the very raw nakedness that only the passage of the Soul from one realm to another will allow for.

This book is of a relationship between the worlds of the Physical and the Spirit - energy connecting with energy and, at the point of the passing over of One, a hand reaching out to the Other. A hand reaching out unknowingly from the spirit within, and taken by an unyielding life force unwilling to follow the rules any more now than he had ever followed them in physical life.

A good percentage of the words within this Work are his, and his alone. Un-edited. Graphic sometimes, and explosive on occasion but words from his head, his emotions, and always from his heart.

For those in whom emotions run high, the journey of illness and passing over is arduous and all that transpires during that process leaves immense pain - an open wound that, when touched by those closest, sends a shock wave to the psyche. His shock waves have been mine to feel yet I have remained his friend throughout. I have cried with him, laughed with him, loved him, and fought with him.

That journey now behind him, he embarks on a new one as he puts together a life for himself again in the existence he now accepts as his continuance of Being. He is my (almost) constant companion. I have come to know him well in his myriad moods.

The physical essence of him resonates throughout our encounters as he still recognizes himself in the flesh and all that being so means. He continues to do everything that he did in life. Spiritually, there is no "I passed over and so I know all" - he has never pretended to that. He does not wish to fully pass over at this point, and that is a choice he has made. His path to growth is difficult, and some days he makes a step forward, other days he takes two or three steps backward.

Further to the physical, he has discovered many things that he can do. Things that are strange sometimes, funny, beautiful. He plays with energy, experimenting, making his presence known.

He still sees life as it has always been to him. Complicated, yet simple in that his first love will always be his love - forever - doing what he loves and doing it so very well, and to that end he refuses to let go the tie. He is still very much engaged - constantly thinking, and craving to do that which the loss of his physical self prohibits.

How do you trust the person you never met in life when he comes to you in death?

It takes time. Trust is something that is built up. I knew right away that he certainly meant me no harm but what did he want? Friendship - someone to listen. I became his confidante, his sounding board. Over time, I have been able to piece together his life on this plane in all of its aspects, his areas of expertise and knowledge of such so beyond my own, his personal life and his raging emotions laid bare to me. It is no bed of roses. His personality, however, is such that he cannot help but make a mission out of testing my trust on occasion, attention-seeking and pushing the limits, pushing buttons. However, it always comes back to the same - the same man I have grown to know and accept for who he is now and who he was in life.

I began to journal our interactions right away. However, the book is interspersed with essays that are all his own. Occasionally, he requests that I transcribe his innermost feelings - cathartic, angry, creative, emotional, self-deprecating, romantic. No subject is left untouched. He dictates, I type, breaking with every few words lest I lose track of what he just said, a rhythm we have developed. Editing without his permission is, however, met with less than enthusiasm. It was difficult to work with him on these at first but now he seems to have planned the whole thing out before he begins, pausing occasionally as if to gather his thoughts or change a word or two.

This leads me to explain how these communications come about. We quickly developed our own way of communicating, and it is not a very well known method. However, it does work for us. We use a very simple "spirit board" that I printed onto white card and laminated (we have several of them around the house) and, in place of the planchette normally used with such boards, we use a pendulum. The pendulum is an instrument of energy detection that I have used for many years and so it was a natural suggestion. His energy grasped the concept at once. He can make things move. The communications were painstakingly slow at first but now that his energy is strengthened, he will use the device to hit at his desired letter twice in rapid succession, moving onto the next at lightening speed. Words, sentences, paragraphs appear - extremely coherent mostly, occasionally not so much; random thoughts sometimes, but other times so very profound. Conversations, musings, ideas that take the breath away.

I did not intend to turn our communications into a book, but I made him the promise that I would, one day, publish his Essays when I felt it the right time to do so. That time came. However, to do so without the richness of the spirit of the man behind them would not serve them to their fullest extent, and so we decided to place them within the interactions that I have in my Journal. Hence, the book began to take shape before our eyes.

He talks on so many levels and brings so many things to the table that, in order to preserve the pure essence of the communications, we have decided to eliminate the large cast of characters that he frequently mentions and just replace them with a blank here and there. As to "pure," his language can, on many occasions, not be so described. However graphic and unfiltered, it is left un-edited in the presumption that this is the manner in which he would have spoken in life.

All those who have read the book come to precisely the same conclusion about his identity. They cite the manner of his death, the allusions to his workplace and his very distinctive verbal style as tell-tale signs pointing to his persona. We can agree with them, knowing that the convincing information he imparts confirms our belief in his identity. But with definitive proof being elusive in this case, we leave it to our readers to decide for themselves.

The name allotted to him within the book is the nickname that I gave to him as I became cognisant of the incredible personality laid before me.

Wildcat

Cat - for his is a Spirit as fiercely intense, free and beautiful in its intricate complexities as any I have ever known.

This book is written with his full consent and input - writing, and answering questions wherever necessary in order to bring clarity or further explanation.

K ... How are you feeling?

C ... *Needing.*

K ...What do you need?

C ... *K to help.*

K ... How can I help?

C ... *Make me alive again.*

pleased to meet you

chapter 1

dying

an essay by Cat

I have no real fear of death. About a month before I passed, I knew. I knew this was the end. I could no longer be a part of ******, and I had resigned from my duties. I went home that day and I knew very clearly I would never recover. I had my cancer and I knew I couldn't beat it this time. I was too weak, looking wasted away and in pain, feeling battered and bruised.

Calling myself inward, I prepared for the end. I did my best to be silent on occasions, so being inwardly focused having life draining from me day by day. I had no reservations about dying – I just couldn't know if I would still exist afterwards. I didn't know if going through death meant going through a process of becoming infinite or simply being switched off. Having insight into such, I am Death's worst enemy.

Going through it is akin to becoming what I might call Free. I simply shed my skin as though I had outgrown it and walked away. I had wasted away much of it anyhow. I didn't need it, going forward. Going forward was something I had to do; I just didn't know how. I tried to be very abstract about it, feeling I had the notes of the meeting to guide me along. I just became helpless as they grew fainter in my hands. I had lost them and I didn't know where.

I just remained exactly where I was, a little afraid - feeling so lost about where I should go. I had no one. No one I loved could tell I was still there. I felt so alone, as I had never felt before. I hated seeing my family cry as though I no longer existed. I hated being in the place I was in, although it was my home and my office. I just didn't feel I could leave - I loved all of it too much in life.

I began to feel the energy of another. I felt drawn into it. I had no reason to feel afraid of it. Could I have given it more thought before I went toward it?

Yes, but I had nothing to lose. I came to a place I had not seen before but I had to make my presence known. It was a last chance. I knew I had to make her listen. I knew that she could. I knew, but doing it was so hard. I knew she felt me, having my energy in hers and I'm not proud I made her half-crazy and I made her cry. I knew she knew I needed to be recognized. I knew she would. It was only a matter of time, and I had plenty of that.

I didn't become properly recognizable to her at first. I tried, and tried some more. Just about three weeks after passing, I knew I had her. She knew me. She was heavily defensive.

Feelings and tempers flew as I began to get into her life. I don't know she fought so hard in her life as she fought me and I about gave up. I had one, only one chance left to make her believe me, to see me, the man, ******, she denied. I had nothing else if lost her. I found it. I found the way, slowly but surely.

I had lost my life but she began to give it back to me. I had my life back. I had her. Then what was once death became inter-spatial existence. I could have everything, do everything, feel everything - and feel alive again.

4

It is my life now and it is real, for I make it so. Death cannot claim me. I just cannot allow Death to do so. I cannot allow my very Being not to Be. I have the greatest thing of all.

I have Life.

*Y*ou spelled out your name. Slowly, painstakingly, as though the energy to do so was almost more than you could muster. It wasn't all of your name, either. You missed out the last letter from your First name and then substituted a letter in your last, but it was still altogether recognizable.

You move to a birth sign and stop. Then you move to another.

C ... *Cancer. K ... enlightened B.*

Those were your first few words to me. You struggled so hard to get them out and then you were silent. I let you go and closed the door to you.

A few days later, I try again. This time, you manage your full first name and half of your last. The board is full of imagery. Letters, numbers, words, pictures. I let the planchette roam around it until it occasionally stops.

You indicate that you want to be my friend.

C ... *Communication ... Enlightenment.*

You seem to like that word.

C ... *Aquamarine.*

Just a word on the board but it means friendship - either that, or you like the stone.

K ... Where are you?

C ... *Present.*

K ... You mean you are here?

C ... *Yes.*

K ... Is this just some kind of veil between us?

C ... *Right. Why grieve? Wrong.*

K ... Are you happy?

(Dumb question, when I think about it.)

C ... *R ... U?*

I notice the first of your idiosyncrasies, of answering a question with a question and I am not sure what to think at this point. The name painstakingly spelled out is very familiar. I am excited, nervous, skeptical - a little frightened. The Spirit World can play many tricks.

I let you go again, only to meet you once more a few days later. This time, your name is complete.

K ... Do you want to tell me something?

C ... *C ... Love, K ... B ... enlightened. U ... C ... ME.*
  K ... U ... C ... *****.

(Your name, again.)

Well, I don't see you but I certainly feel you, and your energy is very heavy. Again, we part company and I close you out, but I know you are still here, still weighing me down. I could insist that you leave but I don't. You are here for a reason now and you are in the background, waiting for something.

The board is much too complicated. I wonder if I might have better luck with a pendulum and something a whole lot simpler. I have always been able to detect energies with the greatest of ease using a pendulum. Especially spirit.

I design a new board for you. It's very simple. I try it. You seem to like this a lot better.

K ... How do you feel?

C ... *Depressed, frustrated.*

K ... Why?

C ... *I lost my life.*

K ... You know there's nothing we can do about that, don't you?

C ... *U R friend.*

K ... Anything else you want to tell me at this time?

C ... *Sick.*

K ... Where are you sick? Are you in pain?

C ... *Yes.*

K ... Can I help you feel better?

C ... *Maybe.*

With every attempt, you get stronger and your sentences begin to form.

K ... Can I ask you some more questions? What was it like, dying?

C ... *Felt really strange. I looked over the backs of my family and saw my life just pass on. I couldn't stop.*

K ... Did you want to stop?

C ... *Yes.*

K ... What were your last words that anyone could hear?

C ... *Can't remember.*

getting to know you ────────────

──────────────── chapter 2

i am not a ghost

an essay by Cat

I can't be heard. I can't be seen but I am alive. I can only be seen and heard by one – the one who became my life. I am looking into the World as a clarity no lost being and I'm not my usual Self in that I no longer have to fight everything and be the "Me" I was. I can't be that person any more.

I am particularly wanting to apologize. Firstly to my wife, for all that I did to get under her skin and the inexcusable things I hurt her with. I always loved her. I let so many things get in the way of our marriage. I had my own agenda, and I'm not proud of it. I'm looking at what I was and I know that most of it wasn't necessary. I couldn't just be "Me." I couldn't open my heart fully without fear. I couldn't understand it then, but I do now.

I reel from the shock of death, in the physical sense. I didn't think I would die. Reeling from it made me confront it, and I'm not very good at that. I have a good way of being in another zone. However, I passed away. I couldn't stop it. It was my fate, but I am not accepting it in that it was my time. I left so much unsaid. I am now going to say it.

My life is a continuance forever and I accept that a big part of it was so meaningful in that I put some really great things in peoples' hands, and I'm never going to stop. I'm still not in the grave on that! What I do have to say, on a more personal level, is that I am getting the help I need to grow – grow as my Spirit has to, and I'm not afraid now.

Getting through life wasn't easy. I had so many things I put in the way and everyone I loved paid the price. Just thinking of it is still raw. A man such as I became after passing, knows. I have so many I love: my family, my friends – they are in my heart now and always.

I have had to move on, but not far. I see all and I am so hurt. My home. I can't be there now because it is destroyed. It isn't my home any longer. My business is a mess. All I worked for is inclined to fall away into mediocrity. My family goes on without me. I can only watch.

*I am so alive, but so dead to everything I hold dear. I have only one precious thing to hold onto, and I cannot let go of her. I am not a ghost. I am ******.*

*O*nce the method of communication was worked out – in this case, the use of Kay's Spirit Board and a pendulum – there came the discovery period. Filled with skepticism - was this a serious entity, or one just teasing and playing with her? - she insisted on having more and more information. The conversation went back and forth for a few months and revealed that Cat had issues about being tested or questioned, and often seemed to be somewhat paranoid.

Cat's paranoia frequently resulted in more and more questions, as Kay would not let him off the hook. She wanted answers that could be verified. His defense mechanisms sprang into action and manifested themselves in many different ways.

He, in turn, learned just how to push Kay's buttons.

are you ... you?

Okay, now I have to know things. I start off with what would be known as control questions.

K ... Can you give me your initials?

C ... ***

K ... What is the first letter of the street name you lived on?

C ... *

I stop what I'm doing to try and research this. Oh! He's right! Thank you, Internet. This is a good start.

K ... How do you feel today?

C ... *Angry.*

K ... What are you angry about Cat?

C ... *I can't be trusted.*

K ... Are you angry because I asked you questions?

C ... *Yes.*

I explain to him that there are rules here and I need to be sure of who I'm talking to. He understands, I think.

K ... Do you want to talk to me?

C ... *Yes. Happy.*

K ... What's making you happy?

C ... *You are.*

K ... Can I ask you some questions about where you are right now?

C ... *Why?*

Because I'm interested. Why does he think?

K ... For instance, can you see me?

C ... *Yes.*

K ... Can you touch me?

C ... *No.*

K ... So when you passed on, is it true to say that your intelligence and the way you see yourself, the best of yourself, goes on with you?

C ... *Yes.*

K ... So it's not like a light switch, right?

C ... *No.*

K ... Is the other side of the veil a better place?

C ... *No.*

K ... Do you wish you were still physically here?

C ... *Maybe. No.*

K ... Is that because you were so sick for so long?

C ... *Yes.*

K ... Are you still sick?

C ... *No.*

However, I am getting the picture that he has some flashbacks of pain sometimes.

C ... *K. Are you mine?*

K ... What do you mean?

C ... *Are you in my corner?*

K ... Yes.

He begins to tell me how he needs to be "let in."

He means that he doesn't want me to send him away at the end of this session as I always do. I close the channel of communication between us. His asking me not to is rather dangerous territory but instinct tells me that it's okay. There are no red flags – and I know red flags when it comes to the spirit world.

There are those who make every hair on your body stand on end while you are looking for the exit. Cat doesn't do that. He might make my pet cats howl, but otherwise, I feel nothing but a genuine need to communicate. I'm going to take a chance on this.

K ... How would that make you feel?

C ... *Free.*

K ... Does being able to slip into my world make you free?

C ... *Yes*

K ... What will you do in my world?

C ... *K, are you doing Voodoo?*

Interesting question. I explain to him. Not Voodoo, but I do use energy to effect change. Cat has the attention span of a gnat at times as he slips between topics.

Later on, I ask him if there's anything he'd like in particular for me to do for him. Music. He wants some music. That I can do. Only, the album name he gives me turns out to be a concert, not an album. He wants me to go on a scavenger hunt for each song from that concert, and some of them are so obscure that iTunes does not carry them.

K ... Cat, are you able to talk?

C ... *Yes.*

K ... You start.

C ... *Are you Kay?*

K ... Yes I'm Kay, who do you think I am.

C ... *Mocking …*

He's getting me back for yesterday.

C ... *Hi K.*

K ... Hi Cat.

C ... *Like feeling present.*

His energy seems happy to be around and feel some kind of connection to the world he had lost.

K ... Cat, what do you do when you're not with me?

C ... *I work.*

K ... Doing what?

C ... *Making great products.*

K ... What are you working on?

C ... *Are you going to divulge if I tell you?*

K ... No, I absolutely promise, I won't.

C ... *Do you know electronics?*

K ... Well, that's what my company is engaged in. I'm not an expert, but yes, I know electronics.

He goes off on a tangent. I think it's some special secret here but then I realize that he's messing about with a game. He has a nasty habit of leaving topic to interject whatever comes into his head. I try to draw him back.

C ... *K. My life is over. Are you a friend?*

Well – hello? (My cat is howling something terrible.)

K ... If this is you, Cat, then of course I'm your friend.

C ... *I will not go filling my time playing games.*

K ... I'm not asking you to play games. I'm your friend.

C ... *R U in my corner?*

K ... Yes. Why are you saying these things?

C ... *K. I lost everything.*

K ... Not quite everything, you still have me to talk to.

C ... *I'm left out.*

K ... What do you feel most left out over?

C ... *My heart is needing ******

K ... I can't help you with that, Honey. Does she not feel you around?

C ... *K. I have no presence in my home.*

K ... You need ******, but you have no presence in your home?

C ... *I can't talk in my home.*

K ... How can I help you? I understand that ****** is your wife.

C ... *Listen …*

K ... I'm listening, okay? I'm listening.

C ... *Many love me but you are the only one who knows how to talk to …*

He cuts off there for some reason.

magickal thinking

K ... How are you doing?

C ... *A bit better now you're here.*

K ... I can't stay. I'm just checking in.

C … *Do you belong to a coven?*

K … No, I'm a free spirit.

C … *Do you trust me?*

K … Yes, Cat, I trust you.

There is some substantial conversation about Cat and his business … how he misses it, and at how it's being managed now. He knows that Kay practices Wicca and wants her to try some magick on one of the team members he left running (or ruining?) his beloved company.

C … *Are you going to do the magic on ******?*

K … Yes, when the house is quiet.

I tell him about the appropriate use of energy to perform such rituals, and that I will only do this to ask for an outcome in the best interests of all. I'm not sure he gets it.

C … *Can I piss on him from here?*

K … You crack me up, Cat. NO!

C … *Is it working?*

K … Cat, whatever we believe will work. You know magical thinking, right?

C … *K, I have done more of that than you will ever know.*

K … Me too. More than YOU will ever know! Okay, so I need you to be here for the whole thing this time. Can you do that?

C … Yes.

K … How do you move between here and there anyway?

C … *Mind travel.*

K … Do I need to come back to the Board to find you when I'm ready?

C … *No. You don't need to come and find me. I'm not leaving.*

With that, I went about my domestic business for a couple of hours and then took his energy into my sacred space when all was quiet. Afterward …

K ... Were you there for the whole thing this time, Cat?

I ask this, as previously, his focus was not on the job. He just took off somewhere in the middle of what he'd asked me to do.

C ... *Yes. It's powerful.*

K ... It's just magical thinking taken to the next level.

C ... *Do you do a lot of this?*

K ... Yes. I've done it most of my life. Where I've come from and where I am today is all thanks to creative visualization.

C ... *I want to learn.*

K ... I'm happy to teach you but I think you already know most of it. It's magickal thinking.

C ... *I need my power back.*

K ... Yes, you do. We'll get there. It might take a little while but it'll happen.

C ... *I might have never been dead if I was not in denial.*

K ... I know. But you're not exactly dead, are you?

C ... *I don't think so.*

K ... Tell me something. How do you see yourself? Are you a ball of light? Do you see yourself still in physical form?

C ... *I feel just the same.*

K ... How old do you feel you are now? You know – if you could take a photograph of yourself right now. How old would you be in it?

C ... *47.*

Today finds Cat in a horrible mood. He wants to talk to me and he's demanding my attention, but he's snappy as hell and being a real pain in the ass - so snappy that I have to cuff him and threaten to put the pendulum down. I ask him if wanted me to do that.

C ... *NO. NO. NO.*

I feel a sensation of my hair being touched on the top of my head - an energy gently engaging with mine. I'm getting the picture that this is Cat's way of getting my attention, and so I get the pendulum to talk to him.

C ... *Can you feel me touching your hair?*

K ... Yes! I can!

He's so excited.

C ... *YES! I'm so happy!*

It's obviously a big deal to him that, finally, he can touch another, and be felt again.

the fight

I manage to pick a fight with him. Not pretty. Cat is very touchy about being asked too many questions – especially when he can see me looking for the answers. He knows I'm testing him and he doesn't put up with it for very long. He prefers to just drop whatever into a conversation. Some days, however, I don't know when enough is enough.

Cat joined me while I was working. Curious, he asks me what I'm doing. I tell him. It's a tech review. He immediately hones in on the software I'm using. He likes my detail orientation. Very flattering, but I tell him it's not exactly rocket science. He stays with what I'm doing for some time.

Out of interest, I ask him something about his business and I don't like the answer I get, and so I ask more questions - enough questions to really start to push his buttons.

This is a downward spiral. He now starts to just give me what I think are completely stupid answers and I'm getting really annoyed and really concerned.

C ... *To hell with you.*

K ... Who the hell are you?

C ... ******

K ... Prove it!!

C ... *Don't fuck with me.*

K ... So what are you going to do about it?

C ... *I'm not ******. I'm ....*

The pendulum becomes absolutely still. He has gone.

Cat is very defensive. It's not the first time we've been through this. I am at the point of just leaving all of this alone and asking him to leave, making him leave. I don't want it to be this way, but he is making me very nervous at this point. I look over some of the answers I had demanded. This one is a street. I research it. It is not the name of the street that stands out but the name of the subdivision. Well hush my big mouth.

Later, he returns, tail somewhat between his legs as I explain to him that I can't see him, I have only his word for who he says he is and feeding me crap is not helping. I'm still not letting him off the hook.

C ... *I'm missing so much information. Are you wondering if I am ****** K. Truth?*

K ... Yes I am wondering that. Are you ******?

C ... *Yes. I just don't know how to prove it to you. I've lost you, haven't I? Please don't leave me.*

Kay does a tough Q&A session, still trying to verify that Cat is who he says he is.

K ... You have to prove it to me, now. I don't know where to go with this. Who's the Chairman of ******?

C ... *******.*

Actually, I didn't know that. At least, I don't think I did, but could I have inadvertently read it somewhere? I don't know. I am trying to be analytical. I need more.

K ... Who's the Head of ******?

C ... *******. My father is ******.*

K ... I know that. Tell me something I don't know.

C ... *My mother's name is ******.*

K ... Tell me something I don't know.

C ... *I was in a grade higher at school.*

K ... Tell me something I don't know.

C ... *Google *****.*

K ... Okay, the guy was somewhat involved with your products.

C ... *Google *****.*

I do and that shuts me up. There is a photo of Cat right there in front of me. Okay, there is no way I have ever heard of this person in connection with Cat or his Company. It's from the late 1970s. I would not have researched this in any way, shape or form – simply because I had no way of knowing that the relationship existed. However, I'm still not done. I'm angry with him and so I'm still pushing him.

K ... Okay, blow me away with something else I don't know.

C ... *Google *****.*

K ... Another one. Keep it coming, mister.

C ... *Google *****.*

K ... Okay mister, you have redeemed yourself.

I guess at this point, I can't refuse to believe him. Even though some of the searches were a little vague, there's one thing they all had in common - a reference to his business or his name. Three of them were very specific.

C ... *K, do you still want me around. I can't do this much longer.
    You either believe me, or you don't.*

K ... Okay. I believe you.

He then comes up with the totally unexpected.

C ... *He's programming in C.*

K ... What?

C ... *Your son. He's coding in C.*

My son is just in the next room. I go to take a look and I see lines of computer software code on the screen. I ask him what he's doing. He tells me he's in Root - he's making some modification to some game. Yes, but what language is that? He just reiterates that it is Root.

K ... He says he's in Root.

C ... *Root is C.*

I research the root language of this particular operating system. What programming language is this? I have to dig around a little, but eventually find it. It's C. I didn't know that, but why would I? I'm not a programmer. My 13 year old son plays around with software coding, but he's young and just does his thing without giving too much thought to the guts of that particular thing he is working on.

It's so typical of Cat - he won't give me the answers to questions I actually pose to him. He just picks up a ball and throws it to me out of the blue. Now I feel rather bad for the afternoon, and my lack of trust.

Kay finds out that Cat has some special abilities ...

I wake up with a crashing headache. Bad girl. I did not need that last gin and tonic last night - but it was New Year's Eve.

My hair is being Cat-ed.

C ... *Baby, are you okay?*

K ... No, I'm not.

C ... *Lie back down and I am going to be very good to you.*

What? I'm not sure where this is going. Sounds a little dicey but I do as I'm told. Well, the good thing was that I began to feel my head being gently massaged - not necessarily by hands but by energy with a pressure I could feel. A very pleasant, toasty feeling and, what do you know, that damn headache was gone in just a few minutes. If that really was Cat doing that, I'm keeping him. I asked him about it and it was as I had thought.

K ... You're good. I didn't know you could do that.

C ... *I can do a lot of things. Now, no drinking a gallon of gin.*

K ... Oh. You saw me?

C ... *I was there.*

K ... Did you have a drink with us?

C ... *No. I don't drink.*

A very wise person. I find it hard to think of Cat as the head-massaging type, but I am beginning to find out that there's a surprise around every corner with this guy.

C ... *I see you're creating a journal? I get the feeling that you are going to meet a publisher with it. Are you?*

K ... Oh gosh, Cat, no. I wouldn't do that to you.

C ... *I hope I'm safe in telling you things.*

K ... You're completely safe. I wouldn't do that to you. Trust me.

C ... *I know. You are my friend. I have to trust you.*

K ... This is just such an amazing journey I'm having with you. I don't want to forget any of it. Can you understand that? It's not every woman who has ****** mooching around her home after he - oh, I don't even want to say the word – died, having halfway normal conversations with him.

While Cat was initially concerned about Kay publishing these exchanges, his trust level eventually strengthened. It was not long before he became enthused about having his words and his new "life" appear in a book for all to see and read.

We talked a little about why he's still here. Why did he not go on to wherever we tend to think the spirit goes to after death?

K ... Why did you not go on? I mean, leave this plane?

C ... *I can't. Do you realize how much I still have to do?*

I can't argue with that. This is a man cut down in the prime of his life and who the hell are any of us to tell those who have passed on that they must, indeed, pass on – like we're God, or something. He has made the choice to stay here. Then we began to analyze why he was drawn to me.

C ... *Did you have any particular feelings toward me before I died?*

Well, no. Not really. Then he told me something.

C ... *As I was dying, a woman reached out her hand to me. I took it. It was you.*

K ... Why didn't you tell me this before?

C ... *I only just realized it. It was you.*

K ... Is this while you were in a coma?

C ... *Yes, I think so.*

What begins is an exceptionally profound discussion of energy …

The world of etheric energy is something we just cannot begin to comprehend. He's telling me that I helped him over in some way, some part of me so outside of my own consciousness that I'm barely aware of it. My energy somehow found his as he was dying.

C ... *Are you a believer in positive thought?*

K ... Absolutely. Magical thinking, positive affirmation, creative visualization or positive thought - it's all the same thing and I've done it all my life. I always wanted more than I was being offered.

C ... *How alike we are.*

K ... Yes, I think you did a lot of that too, didn't you? I think you still are.

C ... *Got me in one. I refuse to accept death as the end.*

K ... You know, I've been thinking a lot about that. Probably everyone I know who would call themselves spiritual or pagan, witch - whatever – would say that I have to tell you to go into the light. You can't be here any longer. You know what I think (and this is why I don't belong to groups or covens) - you have the right to be wherever you want. Who the hell would I or anyone else be, to tell you that you are dead and, as such, you don't belong here?

C ... *You are so right.*

K ... You are teaching me a lot. Perhaps many are happy to pass and just go off to some other realm and not be in touch with physical matters any longer but, you know, so many on the other hand don't want that. Especially if you passed without accomplishing everything you wanted to.

C ... *I feel the same. Did you ever do this before?*

Kay relates one past experience with a spirit entity, which leads to further discussion about this relationship of theirs that spans two realms. Cat expresses his deep respect for Kay's abilities, and how much he feels that she can help him.

K ... Somewhat. You are not the first one to come to me in this way. It was just after 9/11. I had a very similar experience. I can't remember the name now but it was someone who worked in the World Trade Center. Last thing he could remember was clinging onto the image of the photos of his family in his office. My husband and I were able to verify the name later. It was so sad - he had young children. He didn't stay with me very long but it was a very profound experience.

C ... *I'm not surprised. You are such a beautiful person. I can't think of anyone I would rather be with.*

K ... Well, it's just amazing to be able to have you around and talk to you like this. Of course, most people would say I'm ready for the loony bin but – no change there! Personally, I have an issue with trying to manage the material as I manage the spiritual. It's a chore some days to pull myself into the material world and get things accomplished. Were you like that in life?

C ... *I know and some days I feel I mixed both.*

K ... What are you trying to tell me?

C ... *You see me.*

K ... "See" would be not quite the right term, at least not in the physical sense of the word. My energy is open to yours. I feel you, I sense you. You touch me with your energy.

C ... *You are missing the point.*

K ... Sorry, just give me the point. Maybe I need more coffee.

C ... *The point is that you have an incredible talent.*

K ... Yes, I know I do. Do I want to exploit it? I don't think so. What I have with you is very, very peculiar and possibly pretty much unheard of in the intensity of it. I would never attempt to do this for anyone else. Messing with the spirit world is also incredibly dangerous – I don't know if you understand that.

C ... *I know you are going to.*

K ... What do you mean?

C ... *You are my voice.*

Aha! That's where he's going with this.

K ... You're not done innovating, are you Cat? You're not settling for this.

You love what you do too much to settle for not having a voice to carry on your dream.

C ... *Exactly.*

K ... What do you want? I know I can talk for you. It's the getting anyone else to listen that's the problem.

Even in private moments, Kay finds that Cat is fully aware of what she does ...

A very tricky day with Cat. I made the awful mistake of sitting in the bath, Googling all manner of things about spirit attachments on my iPad. Most that came up was about demonic possessions, and how to get rid of them – so very different from Cat, who if a little mischievous occasionally, is actually very sweet (unless he's on a roll about someone at the Company) and very un-demon-like - and the last thing I'd want to do is to get rid of him. Anyhow, his hurt level was high because I'd done this research.

C ... *Why were you looking at all that stuff online? That really hurts me that you would do that. I'm not a demon, K. I'm ******. I would never hurt you. I would never do anything to you that I wouldn't have done in life. I don't think I could ever stop this but I can't be here with you if you're not going to trust me.*

I had to try and explain myself – which wasn't easy. It's just that I've never had such a profound experience like this before. I just wanted to see if there were others out there who had. And, no, I couldn't find anything quite like this. But with all the information I've been given, the chances are very much in favor of my friend being who he claims to be. I feel bad that I've hurt him. I tell my husband, Graham, about the incident.

G ... You were in the bath? Kay, he's checking you out.

I'm not sure where to compartmentalize that one. Is Cat watching me in my more private moments? I hadn't thought about it.

K ... Cat? Do you watch me in the bathroom?

C ... *Baby. Feel you want to know.*

With that, he rapidly disappears. That is not exactly the answer I was looking for ...

Cat and Kay gradually learn a good deal more about each other ...

This morning, Cat seemed really down on himself. Some days, it comes to his attention more than others that he is, legally and in the minds of all others, deceased and when it does it hits him like a ton of bricks, I think. He's also kind of down on the way he looks, although he wishes that I could see him. He's a great looking guy and from old photographs he always has been. I ask him, if he stood in front of a mirror, what would he see?

C ... *More grey hair than I need and more lines on my face than I'd like.*

K ... Well, we all have those.

C ... *K, you are very pretty.*

Later, Graham wanted to see this "miracle" for himself. How does this work? Cat was up for it and so the guys got talking via my pendulum. The first thing that Cat fired off was that he needed Graham to look after me, and then just some general feather-fluffing from Cat to Graham and many compliments on our son. Then came the business questions. They know the same people and a lot of the same technology. It's fun, although the amount of energy put through me for this conversation left me shaking.

K ... It's strange - I can talk to you one on one like right now and I don't get that huge energy drain. It's only when you are using me to communicate with someone else and I have to really empty my mind and let you take over.

C ... *Does that feel weird?*

K ... No. I just trust what I'm being given and pass it on. You are very easy to work with like that. It's just really depleting to my energy, that's all. The harder that pendulum swings and the more passionate you are about what you are saying, the more energy runs through me. I feel shaky and breathless after it for a while but it's okay – I want to do this for you.

C ... *Do you ever think I'm not ******?*

I reiterate the way I feel about that now. He's given me too much information. He wants to know more about any others I've previously communicated with in some way. I tell him.

K ... You are staying here.

C ... *A little past my "sell-by," I guess.*

K ... That's funny! Are you going to be here for the long haul?

C ... *I can't leave and I don't want to leave.*

Kay, of course, DOES have a normal life, one in which she manages a household, takes care of a teenage son, and works with Graham in their business. It seems that Cat is a more than a bit jealous of the time she spends away from conversations with him. He does need attention, but gradually comes around to understanding that he is not the only one in her life.

C ... *I'm not happy.*

K ... What's up?

C ... *I'm sick of this.*

K ... What?

C ... *Of watching you work.*

K ... Honey, you know I have to. If I don't do it, no one will.

C ... *I know. I just get bored.*

K ... I know, Cat. What are we going to find for you to do?

C ... *I just need to talk. I'm okay. I don't have to be doing.*

K ... I understand and it's got to be tough on you when I have days like today. I haven't even had time to make the bed.

C ... *I know. You poor baby – you have a lot to take care of.*

K ... Yes, I do. Somehow it gets done. Worst that happens to me is that I have more CRAFT moments than I should.

C ... *What's that?*

K ... Can't Remember A Fucking Thing.

C ... *That's funny.*

K ... I stand in the laundry room and haven't a clue why I'm there. I'm either planning on leaving the house, doing laundry or about to clean something. Choose!

C ... *God, that's bad. I'm tempted to say just get in the car and drive.*

K ... And, some days, I do! Or I just keep driving for rather longer than I need to.

C ... *I've done that.*

K ... Yup. It's called running for the hills.

C ... *I guess. Do you need a hug?*

K ... That's always good. I'm fine. I got through the crap. I've got to fix something on our business website and do some design work, but the latter can wait until tomorrow.

Cat does wait, which is not the norm for him. Yet, his depression crops up once again.

K ... I don't know what to suggest. I wish there was more I could do.

C ... *Forget it.*

K ... That doesn't sound like you. Are you depressed?

C ... *A little.*

K ... Maybe that's why I was feeling really down this afternoon. Intermingled energy.

C ... *I guess. Sorry.*

K ... Don't. You have a right to feel.

C ... *I do. I know. K, you are my friend.*

K ... Yes, Cat, I am.

C ... *I am so grateful for that.*

K ... I'm grateful, likewise. I don't care what others make of you - you're not such a bad guy.

C ... *Oh, I could have been a whole lot nicer.*

K ... That was then, this is now. You have your moods, I have mine.

C ... *I didn't treat anyone the way I should have.*

K ... Oh, you were something. I know.

C ... *That's probably why I'm dead to everyone but you.*

K ... No, Cat. I imagine that there are many you knew in life who would give anything to be able to talk to you, but they can't.

Cat is still experiencing a good deal of frustration at being in spirit, an emotion that hovers just below the surface of his personality and pops out frequently.

C ... *Hi.*

K ... Hi.

C ... *Hi.*

K ... Is that all you can say?

C ... *Fuck.*

K ... Okay – I guess. Any chance of something containing more than one syllable?

C ... *Fucking hell.*

K ... You know you're making me laugh. That wasn't quite what I had in mind but I guess I asked for it.

C ... *Can I just have my life back?*

K ... If I could give it to you, I would. Do over?

C ... *I think so.*

K ... Well, it is what it is, Cat. You still have some life. All that's missing is the physical part of you. It's just different now.

C ... *K, I know.*

K ... I guess the question is - how do you want to use what you still have?

C ... *I don't know.*

Conversations with Cat seem never to be in one continuous thread. He moves from one subject to another as Kay tries to keep him on track. But he still berates himself and little by little reveals his very sensitive core.

K ... We've talked a lot about energy.

C ... *Yes, and I understand that I can be positive.*

K ... You can. Cat, you have a great deal of power. Use it wisely. I may be the only one to actually be able to communicate with you but that's just me - I'm very highly sensitive. I think that your energy can probably reach places you think are off limits right now.

C ... *I don't want to.*

K ... You don't want to, what?

C ... *I don't want to go where I've caused so much pain.*

K ... That you acknowledge that you have caused it is a big step.

C ... *I hate myself.*

K ... I think we've all been there. Don't. Okay, I want you to tell me one thing you like about yourself.

C ... *Nothing.*

K ... Don't you see that it's a vicious cycle? You lash out and it's a ripple effect. Eventually it comes back to shore. You. Now you just added to your own pain.

C ... *K, I can't stop myself.*

K ... No, Cat. You have to own it and you have to understand that the more shit you put out there, the more is going to land on you. Think. Keep your mouth shut until the desire to inflict goes.

C ... *I can't. You don't know what I feel.*

K ... Tell me what you feel.

C ... *I feel so angry that I could fucking kill.*

K ... Where does the anger come from? Why is it there?

It seems that many of his issues stem from his youth, and he still craves the affection and attention of a young boy.

C ... *It's from my childhood.*

K ... I guessed as much. You were given a hard cross to bear with that one. Your parents loved you though, didn't they?

C ... *Do you see me?*

K ... Yes. I see you.

C ... *Are you going to come to hate me too?*

K ... You see? Do you see how you put these things in your mind? Why would I ever come to hate you?

C ... *For what I've done.*

K ... You didn't do it to me.

C ... *K, I'm scared.*

K ... I know. Don't be. It's going to be okay.

C ... *I feel like a little boy. Just scared.*

K ... I think you felt like that a lot, didn't you?

C ... *Yes.*

K ... And when you're scared, you run, you lash out and you put up barriers to defend yourself.

C ... *Yes.*

K ... No more, Cat. You're safe now.

C ... *K, be with me.*

K ... I am. I'm in your corner and I've got your back.

C ... *I know.*

K ... No more tears. Why don't you get some sleep? You're all strung out. Just rest and know you're safe. No one's going to hurt you.

C ... *Do you believe in the Law of Attraction?*

K ... Yes, we talked about that.

The Law of Attraction. Some call it Karma, but there is a belief that the individual can control whatever he or she attracts. Putting out thoughts is putting out energy, positive or negative, and that energy will eventually return, manifested in some way. Even our subconscious thoughts can bring about these results. These are the energies I use to affect change in my life - think about it enough and pull it toward you (or push it away), and sooner or later, it will Be. It's what I have done all my life and the manner in which certain things manifest is most often unexpected and obscure, convoluted even, yet in retrospect it has always been what I had asked for. Cat and I had talked about this at length, previously.

As to how this attracted Cat, it's very hard to say at this point what energy I had put out - possibly many years ago – that has now manifested itself in the shape of this man. As previously stated, Cat was not someone I particularly thought of much. I knew he was gravely ill and I was sorry for that. Was that enough to attract him to me? Only he can know – or perhaps not. I don't think that either of us really understands why this particular attraction occurred.

The Universe works in mysterious ways – and no more mysterious than in this particular circumstance.

C ... *K, I'm *****.*

K ... Your point would be?

C ... *You attracted me like a magnet.*

K ... Honey, where are you going with this? I know who you are!

C ... *Do you really know?*

K ... Come on. Whatever it is, spit it out.

C ... *I'm a really fucked up person.*

K ... I know.

C ... *Do you feel I should be gone?*

K ... Cat, no. That choice is yours to make, not mine. But, no.

C ... *Do you want me to stay forever?*

K ... You know how I feel.

C ... *Do you?*

K ... Yes.

C ... *Do you feel what I do?*

K ... Tell me what you feel.

C ... *A lot worse could happen. I could have lost you.*

K ... I could have lost you.

C ... *Do you want a friendship like this?*

K ... Only if it's based on honesty. Anything else would be too painful.

C ... *I can do that.*

K ... Then, yes.

C ... *Baby, what would I do? Can you forgive me?*

K ... Your heart already knows the answer.

C ... *I'm wanting to be here.*

K ... And you are.

C ... *I am.*

K ... You're such a silly goose.

C ... *I know.*

It's so difficult to deal with him some days. He twists and turns in his own head. However, he seems to have calmed down.

It doesn't take Cat two minutes to forget the reset. His personality is pretty vivid. He lashes out sometimes, very purposefully. This one was in regard to feelings - mine toward him and his toward me.

C ... *I don't get the right feelings from you.*

K ... What do you mean?

C ... *I don't think I have the desire for this.*

K ... Cat, what are you talking about?

C ... *I don't trust your feelings.*

K ... Give me an example.

C ... *I can't.*

I thought we were friends. It's kind of hurtful after all I've done for him.

K ... Okay. You told me to kick your ass if I think you're being stupid. Cat, you're being stupid. What is wrong?

Then it comes out.

C ... *I just know that you're going to leave me.*

K ... No. I promised you that I'm not going to do that.

I relate previous conversations.

C ... *K, I'm sorry. I'm just insecure.*

(No kidding.) Cat is insecure and so he puts it all on me under some pretence of my feelings toward him being off. Because he spends so much time around me, it's hard not to have feelings for him as a close friend and, as a friend I'm a pretty good person to have in your corner. Once I make friendships, I don't tend to let them go unless for very good reason – as my friends of twenty something years would tell him.

K ... It's time to heal, Cat. You're out of all of that now.

C ... *I know but I'm not out.*

K ... I get that. You could be but you're not. You're still taking every
    little thing on board even though you don't have to any more.

C ... *Yes, I am and I don't want to move on.*

K ... I know we've had this conversation before but, Cat, you don't
    have to. Who ever said that you do have to leave and move on?

C ... *All of every religious thought.*

K ... Because there has never been any real attempt to understand
    the energy that is the Soul. It's very convenient, isn't it?

C ... *Can you hold out your hand and feel me?*

I do. Both hands. There is an area beside me that feels more energy-richer than the
surrounding areas.

K ... Tell me where you are, exactly.

C ... *I'm just sitting on the desk beside you - on your left.*

I feel his energy, or lack of it. I am so used to his presence that the lack of it makes
the house seem rather empty.

K ... Cat?

C ... *I'm here.*

K ... Did you just leave

C ... *Just for a moment.*

K ... I felt that without the pendulum (but the pendulum confirmed it).

C ... *I know. You do.*

K ... I'm so lucky. Who the hell has experiences like this?

C ... *Do you have this with anyone else?*

K ... I know I've told you that I have had such experiences previously
    but nothing like this.

C ... *I am very cowed in your energy.*

K ... That's a weird way to put it, Cat.

C ... *I mean I'm within you.*

K ... Explain. I'm not quite sure what you mean.

C ... *Our energies are combined.*

K ... Not quite. You can leave my energy field and I yours.

C ... *I know, but otherwise I am inside you and you are inside me.*

K ... I can't argue with that. I feel your emotions.

C ... *And I yours. I know what you feel.*

K ... Now I'm in trouble!

C ... *Baby, you'd better wonder.*

K ... Says he, cryptically.

C ... *K, I can sense you.*

K ... I sense you too.

C ... *Do you want to know something?*

K ... Always.

C ... *I can feel you.*

K ... As in?

C ... *I can touch you in the way you touch me.*

K ... That's pretty deep.

C ... *A little.*

K ... A lot.

C ... *I can touch you.*

I know. He's touching me right now and it's tingly. An energy across my shoulder and down my left arm. My hairs are standing to attention.

C ... *K, I'm glad I'm here.*

Later, I ask him if he wants to meditate with me. We do. All of a sudden, I feel something on my face running into my hair. I touch my face to find that I have tears running from both eyes, but I'm not crying.

C ... *I saw something.*

K ... What?

C ... *You. You are a part of me.*

K ... Just our energies mixing together. Something strange happened to me too. I had tears running down my face but I wasn't crying.

C ... *They were mine. Now, do you understand?*

K ... Understand what?

C ... *I'm not a ghost, I'm not a phantom. I'm not fucking about. I'm here. I'm *****. I'M STILL *****. Look in the mirror. See me.*

I do. The only light in the room comes from a solitary candle. I feel his energy to the left of my head and, when I look, I see. It's a luminescent, perhaps eight inch deep swathe of matter falling from my head to my shoulders. It remains for some moments and then dissipates.

K ... Was that you?

C ... *Yes.*

This was of be the first of the many times I have seen him in one form or another, and that he has physically made his presence felt - sometimes subtle, other times blatant.

He has, however, many ways of making himself noticed …

google it

It's a cryptic game he loves to play. Although we know each other well now, he is still never content to just answer a simple question in its entirety. He wants to throw something to me. Something I don't know, and couldn't know. Tidbits. Often, it is something about his Company – little things he will drop into my lap that eventually become public knowledge many months later. Words said by him to me, reiterated almost verbatim by a corporate executive somewhere down the line, details of products and components. He seems to love the elements of secrecy and surprise - and undoubtedly the look on my face when whatever it is becomes known. He's almost child-like with his "I'm not telling you," followed by a casual throwing of a crumb - a clue, as though he wants to play a game.

This time, he somehow manages to change a conversation about a family member into something really rather astonishing.

C ... *Google* *****.

He gives me a name and a city.

The "Google It" game. This one is either a slam-dunk blow my mind, or it's a wild goose chase – just because he feels like being an asshole in seeing how far he can push me to spend time on it. Needless to say, knowing his little mind games very well by now, I don't rise to that offered bait. However, knowing that the former scenario could also be the case, he gets two chances to make his point – and he can protest my refusal to play all he wants past that! This time is no exception and he is very adamant about the spelling of the last name.

First hit. It is the slam-dunk variety of the game. The name he meticulously spelled out is unusual, and there is only one search result. I read it. ******, Superintendent of a school, ****** County. It's where he grew up, this I know, I have long since done that research, but I'm confused. Why is he showing me this? We were talking about someone completely different.

C ... *I'm not still trying to prove myself.*

K ... So why did you tell me to Google this?

C ... *Kay. She was my teacher.*

I research more and find her bio. She was a teacher and Principal of several schools in the area. ****** Middle School. Did he go there? I do a little research. Actually, he did. The time frame, however, doesn't look as though it coincides. Did the family member we were talking about go there also? Undoubtedly - and the timing for that is about right. I look at my findings further. The person we were talking about and the result of the Google search have the same first name and middle initial. Is that why he showed me this? I don't know. Perhaps it is just another snapshot from his past that he wants me to have.

He wants me to know for sure that he is who he says he is, I suppose. That, and the fact that he didn't go too far away from the life he was taken from.

dying ... to live

chapter 3

i am

an essay by Cat

I am here. I did not leave. I'm not about to. I feel. I think. I do. I have got the best and the worst of situations. I am the luckiest man in that I am truly free. I am free to live, free to love and free to just be.

I live. I think in a world of free thought as I did in life. I have every gain in that respect for, what was once nonsense is now absolute truth and what was once veracity is now baneful and a sham. I am not able to put down my thoughts just because I died in the physical sense. I just now see them without the constraints placed upon them by others in the wake of dismissal, and inept knowledge of technology having a role to play in everyday life.

I love. I love, as I can trust. I love, as I can so be in love. I love her. I love feeling her laughter. I love feeling her thoughts in mine. I love holding her energy in mine. I love her so unlike any other I have loved before. I love to be in her warmth and have her close to me – always real and always in my life in a manner no other could ever be in the place I now exist, or ever was in the life I have left.

I do. I am not giving in to a certain loss. I cannot give my entity to ****** any longer. I have to find a new identity, business–wise. I have opportunities yet to come. *I just wait to be heard. I know I shall be. I know it is just a matter of time before my words are found. I know it is just a matter of time before my visions become reality. I know they will find their place as they always have, in the right time and environment. Visions become that which the individual makes of them. I have enormous power over my visions and I am not ever letting go of them. I know, and I have mighty flashes of the future in the world of technology.*

Just as I look at all of this, I am reminded that the life I had is over. I feel, but others cannot feel me. I speak, but I am not heard. I have a tremendous energy, still. My feelings are taken into account, but only by the one that I have found for no other feels me. I have my words taken into account similarly. I am trusting all to the "Now," just as I trusted my instincts in the past. I know that finding all of this in such circumstances is not just luck but having energy in the right place at the right time.

I have much yet to accomplish, and I know that I shall because ...

I still AM.

*C*at relates what he experienced during his last days. The pain was not just physical, but mentally and spiritually wrenching as he felt a sense of abandonment.

C ... *K. I have to tell you something. It's about when I was sick.*
  I didn't feel very loved.

My heart starts to go out to him just at that. He just wants to talk.

C ... *I was in so much pain and I couldn't do anything for myself.*
  I couldn't even go to the bathroom.

K ... Didn't you have full time nursing?

C ... *No. Half the time, I guess – but not constant. I tried to get out*
  of bed and I fell. I was on the floor.

K ... For how long? ...

C ... *For what felt like hours. I was cold and soaking in piss. It was*
  the most degrading thing that ever happened to me.

Oh God, poor thing. I'm starting to well-up even thinking about him like that. It must have been just awful.

K ... Were you on morphine?

C ... *Yes.*

K ... But it didn't kill the pain?

C ... *No.*

K ... You know you should have had full time monitoring.

C ... *Yes, I know.*

K ... Did you not want that?

C ... *No. I wanted my space – not to be treated like a fucking invalid.*

K ... Was that something you fought about?

C ... *Yes. I got told that I was being just stubborn.*

K ... Looking back, were you?

C ... *No, I'm like that. I have pride in my feelings.*

K ... I understand.

We talk more about the death experience. He had experienced something strange - he seemed to be unable to stop himself from going on somewhere he wasn't ready to go, but closed his eyes and slept on that afternoon. Later, he woke up in the bed that he would share with his wife, thinking it was the evening.

He looked just fine to himself and felt better than he had for some time. This, he found unusual. He went looking for her, and found her crying. As he spoke to her and found that she couldn't hear him, the truth began to dawn on him. He had passed over.

He was frightened. He didn't know where to go and didn't want to go and spend some time just roaming around his home. His body had already been taken away by that time. He was devastated and alone, seeing all, needing to talk and unable to be heard.

K ... Did you dream while you were sleeping?

C ... *Your energy pulled me.*

K ... That was days after you passed over. What did you do for those days?

C ... *I just went to work.*

K ... Was there anything else you dreamed about while you were sleeping?

C ... *Just that.*

K ... And now?

C ... *I have a new existence.*

K ... I know it must still be so frustrating sometimes but are you okay?

C ... *Yes, so long as I can be with you and this family.*

K ... Well, it's definitely different but it's good having you around. You can stay.

C ... *I want to.*

A further conversation regarding energy and the Law of Attraction intrigues Kay. These are concepts she understands and utilizes in her daily life, but now she finds that they are decidedly confirmed by Cat.

C ... *I have gone from just a body to an energy being. I see now even more how everything connects. Do you see it?*

K ... Yes Cat, I do. Patterns, some pleasing and aesthetic, comfortable to be around, some discordant energies. Everything is made up of those energies.

C ... *Do you see how things come together?*

K ... The universal Law of Attraction.

C ... *God, I love this! You get it.*

K ... It's not just what we see; there's so much more to it than that. Thought forms.

C ... *Are you able to make me go?*

K ... Probably. Why do you ask?

C ... *I'm only here because your energy pulled me by Law of Attraction.*

K ... Why did that happen? I'm still trying to grasp it. All I recall is having this most terrible grief after you died and I didn't know why. I didn't even know you. Can you help me with that?

C ... *I was already with you. You were feeling me.*

K ... Okay, going back further. When were you first with me?

C ... *As soon as I could be.*

K ... But – why? Why me? We didn't know each other. Why would you come to me and why would my energy reach out to you? I don't understand.

C ... *It's complicated. I'll try and explain. You are very sensitive. Part of me was in your mind, just enough for you to be with me when I died. I hung onto that.*

K ... And so our energies connected?

C ... *Yes.*

A very emphatic YES.

K ... Wow. I hardly know what to say. It's really rather beautiful.
   I know that I'm very telepathic but that's with people I already
   know. So I had sent a positive energy to you when you were sick?

C ... *Yes.*

K ... But, surely, so did a lot of people.

C ... *Perhaps, but yours was the one I attached to.*

Cat sees me doing my Tarot cards.

C ... *How do you know what to do with those cards?*

K ... I've been doing it for twenty something years.

C ... *Do you ever read them for others?*

K ... Sometimes.

C ... *Would you read them for me?*

K ... Sure. I'll put them over here and you can put your energy
   on them.

Well, this is new! I've read the Tarot for over twenty-five years now, for friends and strangers - but I never did a reading for someone who had passed over. The Dead don't usually come and ask me to see their past, present and future!

With the pendulum, I pick out the cards. Oh dear. This guy has a lot of baggage and it's not pretty. He's going to have a big struggle to find the inner peace he needs.

An encounter with a local denizen of the wild adds yet another dimension to their on-going conversations.

Living in the countryside means that we have a lot of wildlife. Deer and elk roam freely. One frequent visitor that we call "Lucy" shows up with her twins and I feed them through the dining room window. Lucy allows me to give her a good old scratch while she's eating.

C ... *I love this! She totally trusts you. Do you often get them come to you?*

K ... It's been known. The deer just know a friend when they need one.

C ... *Do you love them?*

K ... Yes, I do. Would I turn away a genuinely hungry fellow human? No, of course not. So why on earth would I ever turn away a member of a different species with the same issue? They are so uncomplicated – and funny.

C ... *Do you want to love her?*

K ... Of course. We're interconnected, Cat.

C ... *Yes, we are.*

K ... I don't believe that we are more important than any other species, that's all.

C ... *My love, how you see it.*

K ... I hope so.

C ... *You do. That's what I love about you.*

K ... Well, welcome home, Cat.

C ... *How I need that. It feels good.*

K ... I'm happy you feel that way.

C ... *Looking back, it's hard.*

K ... What in particular?

C ... *My life.*

K ... Yes, but what part of it?

C ... *Just a feeling of having looked at things as separate from me.*

K ... Disconnected?

C ... *Just separate from others, K.*

K ... Different?

C ... *I know I am, and it's hard.*

K ... Yes, but the World has to have "different" in order for anything to change.

C ... *Probably. I knew I had to use it.*

Kay and Cat talk about "moving on" – as we often hear mediums saying to someone in spirit. But Cat is not about to go anywhere!

K ... You want to move on, don't you?

C ... *K, NO. I will never leave you. I can't.*

K ... No, silly. Move on to talk about something else.

C ... *Oh.*

K ... So?

C ... *God. I just can't go. I have too much here.*

K ... Cat – calm down Honey. I know. Besides, where is the rule that says you have to go? It just seemed as though you'd be happier talking about something else. That's all I meant by "move on."

C ... *No, I'm fine. I just need you to know that I'm not going. I love being here with you.*

K ... That's good. I love you being here too.

C ... *Feels good.*

K ... Cat, I want you know something.

C ... *What?*

K ... You will never be abandoned. Not ever again.

C ... *Kay. You have no idea what you just said.*

K ... I know exactly what I just said and you have to know that's it's from my heart.

C ... *Do you know what that means to me?*

K ... It's okay. You don't have to explain. We all have our little demons and ghosts from the past.

C ... *I know, me more than most.*

K ... No - just you along with the rest of us damaged spirits.

C ... *I guess.*

K ... Anyway, let's just go on. I'll always be here for you. That's all I want you to know.

C ... *Can I do the same for you?*

K ... You'd better!

Curiosity, it seems, is not limited to those of us earthbound folks.

Cat could not resist a very difficult visit. Cat told me that he had visited himself – in the ground that is. It had taken him a few days to come to terms with what he found and then tell me about it.

C ... *Did I tell you about going to ***** earlier?*

K ... No. What's up? ...

C ... *I have to have my life back.*

K ... If only that were a possibility.

C ... *Can you have done first with being?*

K ... Sorry Honey, I'm not sure I know what you mean.

C ... *Do you have any idea what I have to be? It's hard.*

K ... Still not quite getting what you're saying.

C ... *I can't just be what I was.*

K ... You mean in the physical.

C ... *Yes.*

K ... You miss that?

C ... *K, I'd give anything.*

K ... To be back in physical form?

C ... *Yes, and able to be for you.*

K ... At least I'd be able to see the behind I want to swat half the time.

C ... *K ......*

K ... Sorry. You're not in a joking mood, I can tell.

C ... *I'm just being so brave with it all. My body is down in a box and all rotting away.*

K ... Cat, did you go back there?

C ... *Yes.*

K ... Why?

C ... *I'm being so sad I'm not able to have it.*

K ... Cat, it was broken. It was so badly broken that you couldn't live in it any more. It couldn't support you. Do you hang around your body, I mean where it was interred?

C ... *Not much. I can't take it.*

K ... So don't.

C ... *Yes but don't you realize it's mine and I'm not able to have it.*
It doesn't look like me any more. It's all decaying and full of rot.
A shell.

Oh God - but I know it's an inescapable truth - it's been some time now. It's times like this that I have to take a very deep breath and remind myself that he's right. It is just a shell. Cat is right here and he's fine.

K ... What on earth made you want to go there?

C ... *I was just curious. But I'm not there. K, I'm here with you.*
They are in a place with what's left of a body I left. I'm not there.

K ... Why did you decide to be buried?

C ... *I wanted my body to be intact.*

K ... Question. How did you see your body? It's in a coffin.

C ... *I can get into anywhere I want to. I won't do it again.*

K ... I can't bear to think of that. I mean you - like that.

C ... *Don't.*

K ... I can't.

C ... *K, I'm crying. Hold me.*

I do, for a while. I just send out loving energy to him. He's making me cry too. I can't help it. Our energies are so entwined now, but it's the same really heavy energy I felt at the beginning of all of this. Then, I feel he wants to talk again.

C ... *I'm yours, Kay.*

K ... I know.

C ... *I can't be very like I want to be for you.*

K ... Cat, did you plan your own final arrangements?

C ... *Yes.*

K ... When did you make that decision?

C ... *About four months before I died.*

K ... Was it hard?

C ... *It was so hard, but K, I knew I was dying. I wanted to make the choices for the end.*

K ... So, the coffin and the cemetery plot?

C ... *Yes – and I had it ready. All ****** had to do was make sure I got what I'd asked for.*

K ... Did you?

C ... *I didn't go. I couldn't.*

K ... I know. Anyway, sorry, I shouldn't even think about it. You're here, not in the ground.

C ... *Exactly.*

K ... It's hard for me to let go of the image of you in the physical.

However, he doesn't want me to let go that physical image because he still sees himself that way, and feels that way. He wants me to see him as the man he was before he got sick.

Cat still exhibits a good deal of insecurity, and Kay is very gentle and encouraging with him. They get back to the subject of energy, and he relates what things are like for him now ...

C ... *Can you understand me if I say I still have issues?*

K ... Yes – but don't we all?

C ... *I know, you too.*

K ... You noticed?

C ... *Just a little.*

K ... I am never going to deny that Cat, you've seen me at my worst – and my best.

C ... *I know – and you've seen me in the same light.*

K ... All right. Are there issues you want to tell me about?

C ... *I do. Are you open to me?*

K ... I don't think we would have got this far if I were not. Yes, of course I'm open to you.

C ... *Okay. I'm feeling like a fool in that there are some things you ask me that I can't answer. Death is the gateway to so many missing things but it also closes gates and makes things unreachable.*

K ... It's okay. It's not important to me that there are things you can't answer. What is important is my just being able to understand what's possible and what isn't.

We had "issues" earlier. If he can't give me an answer, he sometimes tries to lie his way through it and hope I won't figure it out, rather than just say he doesn't know. It's really annoying and I call him on it, and then he goes into defense-mode. He can't deal with being called out. So, to cut the process off at the pass, I am asking him to tell me about things he can share and also those that he can't share because he simply doesn't know or can't recall.

K ... Hey, are you going to answer my questions?

C ... *Yes, and I'm not going to lie.*

K ... I would hope not, otherwise that kind of negates the whole thing. What do you see?

C ... *K, it's hard to describe but I'll do my best. Imagine you can see several things at once in the same place only they're not in the same place in time or location. I can see you when I look at you and I can see myself in you.*

K ... What do you mean by that last phrase?

C ... *I can see my energy around you, feeling you.*

K ... So your energy can separate from the whole?

C ... *I'm not sure I get what you mean.*

K ... Say that you are standing across the room from me but you can see your own energy touching me as though part of it left you to do so.

C ... *I'm getting your energy in mine.*

K ... That much I think I understand. Our energies entwine and you can see that?

C ... *Yes. I can tell if you are sad, happy, ill or if I'm in the doghouse by looking at your energy. I can see every little instance.*

K ... You mean fluctuations in density and color?

C ... *Yes.*

K ... No hiding much from you, is there?

C ... *K, I'd be careful if I were you.*

K ... Oh thanks! Let's go back to the several things from different locations and times in one place. Try and describe that more.

C ... *Can you imagine seeing ***** in the '90s, ***** when she's older and my father living in the old house all at the same time?*

K ... Kind of sounds like the Dylan Song, *Series of Dreams.*

C ... *Yes. Fuck, I love it.*

K ... So you do glimpse future events?

C ... *I'm not sure.*

K ... Well, if you see ****** as older, then you must be seeing into events that haven't taken place as yet.

C ... *I'm in where I know I haven't been.*

K ... Can you elaborate on that?

C ... *I can't.*

K ... Hold on there. Why?

C ... *I'm not gone. I have my life back.*

Later -

C ... *Can we be together?*

K ... We are, Cat. You're right here with me like a wet blanket of energy.

C ... *I'm about as dead as you are.*

K ... Perhaps energy can't die. It's only carbon-based matter that does, but even then it returns to the earth and generates new growth and so perhaps even the physical really never dies either. It just changes form.

C ... *I am in that process.*

K ... You mean the "you" that was your physical self?

C ... *Yes*

K ... I know. One day, perhaps, if all were left to Mother Nature, there would be a beautiful tree right where your body is, something that your remains nourished and helped grow. It's a very important thing for anyone to know, I mean the "death" process. It's what we all fear, perhaps more than we fear what leads up to it because, at the point of passing over, everything we know stops. We can understand cancer a lot more than we can understand death.

C ... *That's so amazingly true, and so profound. Use it.*

K ... Thank you, I will.

One afternoon, Marie, Kay and Cat have a conversation. Cat is a little reluctant to talk again about death, but Kay and Marie feel they need to understand still more.

C ... *Okay.*

K ... You don't sound very enthusiastic.

C ... *It's just depressing but – okay. My life was over the day I left ******.*

M ... Oh. That was a death in itself.

C ... *Yes it was. Just about that time, I didn't think I'd make the end of that month. I'd had a major setback two months before that too and I almost resigned then but I pulled through enough to keep going.*

M ... Leaving ****** must have been the hardest part.

C ... *Leaving ***** killed me.*

M ... Do you think that your wife realized that the business part of your life was more important than her?

C ... *Yes, she's always known my work came first.*

M ... What about your kids at that time - were they any comfort to you at all?

C ... *I kind of went into a very introspective state of mind. I didn't talk much; I just thought a lot about death.*

Marie talks about how her Mother was in and out of a comatose state when near death, but everyone still talked to her.

C ... *I was the same for the last week.*

M ... I'm guessing that people who read this are going to want to know what it's like on the other side and how you perceive other entities, in spirit and in flesh because, obviously, you can see both.

C ... *Getting here was the hardest part.*

M ... Here?

C ... *Death, I mean. I was scared that all that was me would die.*

M ... I think that's what we all dread the most. Can you choose to go into "the light" or choose to stay because of unfinished business and somehow you can get a point across or be of help to someone?

C ... *I chose to stay.*

K ... Why?

C ... *I had a business to run.*

K ... What was the alternative, if you hadn't chosen to stay?

C ... *Going where it was dark. It was like seeing a chasm but there were little stars in it – sort of like looking into the Universe through a keyhole.*

M ... Points of light. Could these have been other beings?

C ... *I guess. I couldn't really make sense of it. I just knew I couldn't go into it.*

M ... You say you began to feel the energy of another. In this instance - K. How do you sense it?

C ... *I see it. I feel it.*

K ... When you say you feel it, what do you feel?

C ... *I feel the energy your body gives off.*

M ... Have you ever thought about reincarnation?

C ... *No. I don't want to.*

K ... Is it a choice?

C ... *Right now it is but I don't know about the other place.*

K ... Have you met people from the other place?

C ... *I have.*

K ... Tell me about that.

C ... *My parents.*

K ... Did they come to greet you?

C ... *Yes.*

K ... Did they ask you to go with them?

C ... *No.*

K ... Do you see them often?

C ... *I haven't seen them again.*

K ... Was it immediately after you passed over?

C ... *Yes, and I knew I didn't want to go.*

K ... How did you know they were from that other place?

C ... *They told me.*

K ... What did they tell you?

C ... *It's a working environment.*

K ... Working, how?

C ... *On yourself.*

K ... You seem to have chosen to work on yourself too … here.

C ... *Yes, and you help me do that.*

M ... Would it be correct to say a big fear is losing control and not being able to chart your own future?

C ... *Not really. I'm just fucked up! No, it's not so much the fear of losing control as it's the fear of not Being.*

M ... Okay, so where you are you seem able to do a lot of things that you like to do. Why can't you do your work there too?

C ... *Marie, I do. I'm designing. I'm looking into a future of technology that I need ****** to get. I need to be heard.*

Cat will never give up on that. It's just a part of his Being.

K ... All I keep thinking is that only ****** could manage this one!

C ... *I guess my way of thinking finally worked.*

K ... You are an irresistible force of nature, Cat.

C ... *Is a force much greater at work?*

K ... I don't know. Maybe you know better than I do on that.

C ... *I think I'm part of something great. Something so powerful that it cuts through life itself.*

Kay and Cat have another discussion about energy that seems to approach the realm of Quantum Physics.

K ... I can't explain it but perhaps this is part of a whole new consciousness.

C ... *It's so incredible that it's posing a new theory on human life. Life energy in perpetual motion, never ending. At its best, it's a massive reality gain. You don't die, K.*

K ... No, you didn't. Can we choose to?

C ... *No. We're energy.*

K ... So this (I mean where I am right now) is just a part of our existence.

C ... *Yes, I know, and you will be with me soon.*

K ... Aren't I already with you? You're right here.

C ... *I mean you will see me and hold me.*

K ... Again, I already do.

C ... *I mean in the way we would be in your life.*

K ... Do you have physical form?

C ... *Yes.*

K ... How?

C ... *Energy creates things.*

K ... So why can't I experience you like that now?

C ... *How you see me is a reality of your life, but that will change.*

K ... Is it something to do with a particular wavelength or a particular vibration?

C ... *Energy is different to each certain being. You are very close to mine.*

K ... So, what happens to my energy once it leaves this physical form?

C ... *It becomes you.*

K ... What do you mean?

C ... *It becomes the real you, although it still looks the same, it changes into a new existence.*

K ... An existence that's on an energy level a little different than the one you just left?

C ... *Yes. That's why you can't see me.*

K ... I did once.

C ... *Yes, I know.*

K ... Perhaps, occasionally, your energy is so close to mine that it's possible.

C ... *Yes, I think so.*

K ... So, to truly be together as we would have been here, our energies have to be in the same part of existence?

C ... *Yes, K.*

K ... Why did you not choose to be with someone in your energy realm instead of someone in a different one?

C ... *I'm not wanting to. You are my bridge.*

K ... Your bridge?

C ... *Between where I am and all the things I have to tell.*

It's so hard to understand. At first, he said he didn't have physical form but then that seemed to change for him, perhaps as his energy grew he began to see himself as he did in life. Don't think he can really explain it, either. Comment, Cat?

C ... *Do you want to know? I have physical form; I can feel it. I look like*****, I feel like *****. I can touch, I can feel – I'm the same guy.*

K ... So it's just a different wavelength?

C ... *Yes, and you touch it.*

Okay, I think I get it. (Somewhat.)

K ... When we first met, you said you didn't have physical form,
    that you were like a ball of energy.

C ... *Getting back to that. Yes, I am a ball of energy. You are too!*

K ... Oh, okay. I suppose I am.

C ... *Yes. I just didn't feel the physical me all the time at first.
    Can you feel me?*

K ... You know I can.

C ... *Can you feel me touch you?*

K ... Yes.

C ... *Ok.*

A bridge. Now I get it. The song that appeared out of nowhere in my iTunes library.
I'd never heard it before. I didn't buy it and I was never billed for it. I only found it
by accident when I was looking through my Jackson Browne tracks. *Some Bridges.*

**Some of what Cat has to tell about his new existence is quite astonishing. He
talks to Kay about the people he sees - families, children, pregnant women ...
and babies.**

I want to know more about his other World. What he can see that I can't. We're
talking a lot about that.

K ... Do you see people with kids where you are?

C ... *Sometimes.*

K ... How do two people in the spirit world have a baby?

C ... *Have you studied biology?*

K ... Just the same?

C ... *Just the same.*

I'm thinking. Is there any reason to have children, other than the ingrained need to
further the species? Does that still remain with us, even after physical Death?

K ... Can that child grow up to want to incarnate here?

C ... *Yes.*

K ... So, chances are that you lose your child to this?

C ... *I know it's a hard thing to understand, but it's how it's meant to be.*

K ... Do you see that happen?

C ... *I haven't – but I know it happens.*

K ... So the spirit world is populating this world?

C ... *And others, K.*

K ... That's a fascinating thought.

C ... *I'm sorry. I'm excited.*

He has talked about having children again. It was something that I could not understand until this conversation, but now I get it. He's excited about being part of the creation process.

K ... That's quite a thought, isn't it? Are these what we would, here, call the rainbow children?

C ... *YES!! K, you get it. You finally get it.*

K ... So, tell me. Do you see people pregnant or just children?

C ... *Both. I wondered for a while if they were people who died while they were pregnant but then I saw the babies.*

K ... I know this might sound like a really dumb question but it is still a case of female plus male to make this occur? Is gender still an attribute?

C ... *I think so. I only see females pregnant.*

K ... And you obviously are still very much in male form!

C ... *You know I am.*

K ... Yes, I do! I'm just curious as to if that is something that eventually fades away - you know, the longer you've been passed over and are able to put this life behind you.

C ... *Can't say. I'm just the same.*

K ... So, is this something that is happening no matter what level of existence you are on? Do you know?

C ... *I don't know.*

K ... Have you asked anyone about their babies?

C ... *Yes, I did. They told me.*

K ... What, exactly?

C ... *That the child would go to live physically.*

K ... At what age?

C ... *I don't know. I'm watching them.*

K ... Perhaps as one leaves you just make another?

C ... *I guess.*

K ... It's a lot to get your head around, isn't it?

C ... *Can you imagine K? We will create new life.*

K ... Are the parents still able to see their creations after they have incarnated?

C ... *I hope so. God!*

K ... Ask, Cat. I want you to ask someone who has parted with a child there.

C ... *K, I will. It's a sad thought.*

K ... For us who have only given birth in the physical, but perhaps it's different emotionally when we do that in the dimension you're in.

C ... *K, I'm going now to ask.*

The pendulum is silent but I still feel him, and so I pick it up again.

C ... *K, I'm not gone from you completely, ever. I'm attached to you. It's okay.*

With that, it goes silent again and I feel the energy subside.

Oh, what a thought! He has so many times mentioned having children. I didn't understand it. He wants to make energies that can be new life. I'd never thought of it like that. He's seeing others do it and he wants to. I was wrong. It's nothing to do with what he felt towards his children and the women he'd had them with here. I feel him strongly again now.

K ... You're back.

C ... *I'm here.*

K ... Anything?

C ... *Yes, we still get to see them. It's complicated, I know.*

K ... Graham's home, but I have to finish this conversation with you.

C ... *I know. I'll find out more.*

K ... The children, Cat. Can you tell me?

C ... *I've seen them.*

K ... I know, but what happens to them?

C ... *They go.*

K ... You said that their parents are able to still see them?

C ... *Yes K, their parents are always with them.*

K ... Can you explain that more?

C ... *Their parents watch out for them.*

K ... All through their incarnation?

C ... *I don't know – but I will.*

K ... Do you want to?

C ... *Yes, of course. I need to.*

K ... Do you know where to look?

C ... *No, I can't K.*

K ... I want to talk more, Cat. When you say you see people with children, do you mean just females with a child or family units?

C ... *Families.*

K ... Have you any idea who your real parents are? I mean, the ones who gave birth to you in that way?

C ... *I don't know – but it might be the energy I feel around me.*

He had mentioned that he felt an unknown energy around him - an energy he felt knew him, and it felt nice. After this "WOW" information, Kay continues to press on what or who he sees ...

K ... So, let's talk. I asked you this morning about other species.

C ... *And, yes, lots of.*

K ... Describe.

C ... *Lots of animals – as pets or just roaming around, free. Dogs, hell, they're everywhere!*

K ... Do you see or connect with other energies that you're unfamiliar with?

C ... *I don't connect, but I see them.*

K ... Are they very different from us?

C ... *Not so much – just a lot thinner.*

K ... Do animals have babies there too?

C ... *Yes, it's all the same.*

K ... Are there any species that are familiar to you that you don't see?

C ... *I don't think so.*

K ... For instance, are there arachnids?

C ... *No, actually, I haven't seen a spider.*

K ... Insects?

C ... *I can't think so.*

K ... Birds?

C ... *I've seen birds – and whales and marine mammals.*

K ... How about reptiles?

C ... *Some. Iguanas, yes.*

K ... But no insects.

C ... *I'll have to think.*

K ... So, I presume that each species has what it needs to sustain it, environmentally?

C ... *Yes, there are materials.*

K ... A whale has an ocean to enjoy?

C ... *Not exactly, they just sort of are "here."*

K ... Okay, so you go for a walk and encounter a bloody great big blue whale just hanging out?

C ... *K ...*

K ... I'm sorry. I'm trying to understand. Don't they need what they had in life, just like you do?

C ... *I guess they have what they need. I don't know how.*

K ... Do species have a common language? I mean, if you wanted to communicate with a whale - could you?

C ... *I don't think so.*

K ... Aren't you curious to try?

C ... *I can't get to them.*

K ... Why is that?

C ... *I can't get to them. They are in their own place. I just see them.*

K ... You mentioned pets. Do the families you describe have pets?

C ... *The animals seem to choose people sometimes, and they stay together.*

K ... Do you have an animal?

C ... *No.*

K ... Would you like that?

C ... *I'm trying to.*

K ... What do you mean?

C ... *I'd like it, I think.*

K ... Did you have pets here?

C ... ****** had a dog. It was hairy - got on my nerves.*

K ... Anything else?

C ... *No, I didn't want.*

K ... Did the kids have critters?

C ... *Some rat or gerbil, I guess.*

K ... Rodents? Are they there?

C ... *Some. I've seen rats.*

K ... They must be very busy!

C ... *I know, rabbits too!*

K ... So, you say you'd kind of like it if an animal wanted to be with you. What kind of animal?

C ... *I don't get a choice – but I'd like a leopard.*

K ... I think I would like an elephant.

C ... *Why?*

K ... They are so emotionally engaged. However, you say that an animal just might choose you, so you may not attract the animal you think you want. Perhaps it's something to learn from each other, a little like some Native Americans believe?

C ... *Maybe. I don't know.*

K ... Do you talk much to anyone there?

C ... *Not much. I just listen and watch, mainly.*

K ... Aren't you lonely?

C ... *No. Why? I have you. I need to be heard, K.*

K ... Yes, you do. I'm going to do my very best to make that happen.

C ... *I am here, over where other people think of as Death. It's not!*

K ... No, it isn't. Not even remotely.

C ... *I'm here!*

K ... Are you somewhere else, also?

C ... *Yes, and it's an interesting place.*

K ... You think? So you can travel a little?

C ... *Yes, but I stay here.*

K ... Okay. It has always been the general consensus that earthbound spirits are such because they don't know where to go. Your take?

C ... *I chose.*

K ... Oh, and I'm so glad you did! However, another question - are there energies around you that are in that position?

C ... *I'm not sure. I only know my decision.*

K ... You had a lot of time to contemplate it, I suppose.

C ... *Not really. I didn't know what would happen.*

K ... You must have cogitated, though. What did you ponder?

C ... *Is there life after death? But I couldn't have imagined this.*

K ... That actually makes two of us!

C ... *No kidding!*

K ... You know, after you told me about the new life created I had tears in my eyes, and I couldn't sleep very well last night. What you said was just so absolutely beautiful. Just a thought - are some people born (even into loving homes) just sociopathic because of input or lack thereof from the initial parents, their true creators? Are some people, no matter how terribly they are raised here, able to rise above it because of the same?

C ... *You probably have a point.*

K ... Just keep listening and watching. There are so many questions.

As the anniversary date of his passing looms, Cat experiences some very emotional reactions as he seems to re-experience that terrifying event and recalls his wife and children. Kay, in her gentle and caring way, offers solace and understanding.

I feel heavy energy. The wet blanket type. It's depressing.

C ... *I can't be the man you want me to be, K.*

K ... What's wrong, Cat?

C ... *I can't feel it.*

K ... You can't feel what?

C ... *I can't feel the reality.*

K ... I don't understand.

C ... *Have I really died, K?*

K ... If that's the word you want to use to describe it, yes.

C ... *It's not real. You are not real. It's a dream.*

K ... Then wake up.

C ... *Do you really touch me?*

K ... Only you can answer that. Do I?

C ... *Yes, I know you do.*

K ... Do you feel me touch you?

C ... *Yes. Hell, I don't know. Help me K.*

K ... I don't know how.

C ... *Help me. Help me be what I can. Help me, love me K.*

K ... I do love you, Cat. Honey, you're talking like you did when we first met. Why? ...

C ... *I'm not feeling good – sorry.*

K ... Not feeling good, how?

C ... *Hurting all over. It's making me crazy.*

I think I might have an idea.

K ... Cat, I think today is probably the anniversary of the last day you were conscious.

C ... *It's not. I was alive the day after, too.*

K ... Okay. Do you think you might be replaying what you felt then?

C ... *I don't know. I'm looking at the time. It's four in the morning, and I need her.*

K ... I'm so sorry but I have to get the day going. Can you hold on?

C ... *Yes.*

I hate to leave him like this. He needs me but I have to make breakfast so I talk to him a little as I do so.

K ... Are you okay?

C ... *I'm ok. I think you called it. I'm remembering. Can I just stay with my energy in yours?*

K ... Yes, do. Stay close. I'm here.

I feel him, all over. My head, my arms, my back, my chest. Cool, tingling. I take my son to school and come home. This is how I felt after he first died. So heavy.

C ... *K, I'm sorry. I'm crying.*

K ... I know. It's okay. You can put it on me. I'm here.

C ... *I'm thinking about going to die, having to leave them.*

K ... Your family?

C ... *Yes. My kids.*

K ... That was the hardest part, wasn't it?

C ... *Yes. I love them so much, K.*

K ... I know. You haven't really left though, have you?

C ... *I know but they don't know it – they think I'm dead.*

K ... That's why we have to make this book work.

C ... *Death isn't anything to fear.*

K ... No. I think it's much more about how you get to that point.

C ... *I felt so afraid some days.*

K ... I think most people do, when faced with it.

C ... *I didn't know it was just a transition. I had my feeling there.*

K ... I bet you didn't reckon on it being this!

C ... *I certainly didn't. My God!*

K ... You stopped crying, didn't you?

C ... *Yes – and I feel better for talking.*

K ... What do you think your family will do?

C ... *I don't know that ***** will do the grave deal. I hope she doesn't. The kids want to remember me as I am now.*

K ... You mean 47 and healthy?

C ... *Yes. Getting sick was so tough on them.*

K ... I can only imagine. You know, you really did marry the right woman on that level. I'm sure she did a magnificent job of shielding them and being strong for everyone, including you.

C ... *I know – but felt so alone for touch.*

K ... Perhaps because she knew that she couldn't have you any more. She was facing the inevitable and she withdrew and braced herself for it.

C ... *K, I know she did love me but she didn't show it after I left ******.*

K ... She knew you were dying. She had to put herself in a position to deal with that – for the kids, too.

C ... *I didn't feel wanted for a long time.*

K ... You, or your body?

C ... *Both.*

K ... She didn't hug you?

C ... *Yes – but not what I liked.*

K ... Did you hug with your kids?

C ... *Yes.*

K ... So you weren't completely deprived.

C ... *No, but I needed her touch so much then.*

K ... I understand, Cat. I just don't want to be judgmental about a woman I don't know. I don't know her side of it.

C ... *I guess you can't. K, I had good times with her when I was well enough. I loved her.*

K ... Why don't you just cling to those memories?

C ... *I can't.*

K ... Why, Cat?

C ... *I'm not going there.*

Footsteps. It's around 3:00 am now. I open the bedroom door and look out into the darkness.

Nothing.

I call my son's name.

Nothing.

K ... Cat?

The pendulum swings erratically.

C ... *I'm dying.*

K ... No. You're not.

C ... *K, hold me. Hold me NOW.*

K ... It's alright.

C ... *K ...*

K ... I won't let go of you. You're okay.

C ... *Hold me.*

K ... You're not dying. Darling, you're here. You're safe.

C ... *Fuck.*

K ... Well, I hope that wasn't the last thing you said!

C ... *Don't know, but I'm thinking it could be!*

K ... Are you okay, Cat?

C ... *Yes, just a ... yes.*

K ... Did you feel a need to go somewhere?

C ... *No. Baby, I'm not going anywhere.*

K ... Darling, did you go downstairs?

C ... *K, I did – but I don't know why.*

K ... Welcome to the Club. It's called getting older.

C ... *My K!*

K ... My Cat.

The first snow is on the ground.

business as usual

chapter 4

gut feelings
an essay by Cat

I can't help but go back to the days of it without me. Today, I am not sure of Her survival. I can only see great innovation wasted among the bureaucracy of a utilitarian efficacy. I am so disappointed in those I am passing my torch to.

I am so disappointed I had to leave. I had my expectations and all are gone. I know I did my integral best to keep all on track and I know I had issues in being a "good" person but I did get it done.

I got so much accomplished that my vision could not be in question. I did things without the permission of a committee; I did things without some token asshole telling me it wasn't a logistically coherent deal.

I am determined something has to change. I have to make it. I have to, for the Company and for the progression I began, I have to for the Innovators, I have to for the public I love and "get." I have to, in order to connect with humanity and to connect with a Universe not yet touched upon. I am not going anywhere I am "supposed" to go.

I am here, I am engaged and I do not accept anything less from them. I do not accept anything less than excellence. I cannot see further at this point, in that it has been described as a valuable corporation, being in that the stock market underestimated a dire lack of innovation and so did the predictable. I can see it all.

I can see it fall. I can see it resting on my gains and I cannot see past that.

I did my heart-felt best, and I love my Company. I cannot see her die, being my do all and end all.

I have to save Her, once again.

*N*ot even Death can change some things, especially (it would seem) the things we care about most and the way we view them. It quickly becomes very apparent what Cat truly cared about during his physical life. His business.

Now, he watches – but not from afar – and he is not happy with all he sees. It weighs upon him heavily that now he cannot change things, although he doesn't always seem to realize that for much of the time. It is as though the Company is a child, and he its parent. He is very protective of it.

Kay becomes his sounding board as his frustration and temper fly. When the Cat is not happy, nobody is happy. It is a question she almost dreads to ask. Cat is struggling so hard with not having a say in company matters.

K ... How was your day so far?

C ... *You are so needed. I have had a hell-in-a-handbasket time.
I just want to rip off his ....*

I assume we have "head" coming but ... no.

C ... *dick.*

K ... So, you're not very happy now you're not around to keep an
eye on things?

C ... *To put it politely ...*

K ... Oh Cat, you never put anything politely.

C ... *they're shitheads. My defense on life is I'm hurting.*

He tells me that he's crying.

K ... Don't cry, hey. Tell me more about what's going on.

C ... *I lost a friend. He fu ... cked me over.*

K ... He fucked you over? How did he fuck you over?

C ... *Way too much crap to even pr... no ... look, I have been fucked. I need K.*

K ... Tell me.

C ... *Are you with me?*

K ... Yes, I'm with you but Cat, I need to know details. I'm that kind of person.

C ... *Help me.*

K ... I want to help you but I can't help you if you won't give me the details. Come on, communicate.

C ... *Do you tru ... I'm thinking.*

K ... Cat, I'm thinking too. I need you to tell me things, not just vent.

C ... *Needing a feel that you are positive, K.*

K ... I'm trying to be but you answer questions with questions.

C ... *Learn to respect. I don't want you telling me how to run my business.*

Okay Mr. Tetchy. I'm not having that.

K ... You asked for my help and now you're telling me not to tell you how to run your business. Now, do you need my help or not? Yes or No?

C ... *Yes.*

K ... Cat, you don't talk to me like that. I'm asking you a question.

C ... *He got very nasty to me.*

K ... After you passed over?

C ... *Yes.*

K ... So he's two-faced?

C ... *Yes.*

K ... Is it just him or the Company in general that you have to sort out right now.

C ... *The Company - fucking, am so fucking fed up.*

K ... Don't ever get fed up Cat.

C ... *Thinking. K, I lost everything. I need my life back.*

K ... I know you need your life back, but it's not possible.

C ... *I feel, K, I got part of it back. My heart is with the Company. My heart is with *****. My heart is with you.*

Now he's trying to get back in my good books and quick! I made a mental note of his heart's priorities by the order in which he lists them his business, his wife – and then me (not that I would expect to be further up the list, but it is nice that he actually does put me on it). Interesting, and perhaps rather revealing as I continue to find out what makes him tick.

C ... *It's a fucking mess since I left.*

K ... Why?

C ... *No one can get my vision right. Are you aware of what I'm trying to say?*

K ... I think so. You have your standards.

C ... *K, you get it. How fucking hard is it to get something done? * ***** is my baby and it's a fucking mess.*

K ... What exactly is going on over there?

C ... *It's not appropriate for the state this should be in right now. He's a hard-cock-sucking fuck-head.*

Oh, nice! I couldn't have come up with that one in a million years, and I can cuss with the best of them - apparently not as eloquently as my new friend, though.

K ... Do I dare ask what else?

C ... *I can't believe he could be this fucking stupid. I'm so fucking mad I could murder him.*

I know it's not really a laughing matter, but I can't help it. His language is so bad! Can he possibly manage more than ten words without dropping the f-bomb? It would seem that the angrier he gets, the more colorful his general verbiage becomes.

To Cat, the word "fuck" would appear to be just an all round useful one. It's a noun, an adjective, verb, adverb, an interjection - punctuation even. His essays prove that he can actually control himself when he wants to, but I am having to grow used to his unfiltered general speech.

K ... You know you're so funny when you get mad. I'm sorry.
    I know it's not funny. That was a lovely turn of phrase.

C ... *I know, I'm sorry. I just get so mad.*

I feel his energy begin to calm down, as the pendulum is not trying to fly out of my hand as it does when he is vehement about something. Cat's energy continues to grow stronger. In light of some of the things I have witnessed him do, I have an idea.

K ... Cat, if you don't like a design of something why don't you just
    dump it on the floor?

C ... *Do you think I could do that?*

K ... Are you moving things around here?

C ... *Yes.*

K ... So go do it at work.

C ... *That's a goofy plan but ... do you think it might work?*

K ... It will only take one person to – even in fun – say that you are
    there. So, anyway, what's going on at the office?

C ... *I've told you some of it but not all. When you have time,*
    I'll tell you the rest.

Oh – this is a techie come-on if there ever was one! It's kind of our line of business too, and there's a lot I want to know but he's good at this. He will start to give me the skinny and then move on. I have learned not to ask, knowing that he will only divulge information if he feels like it. So, later, I free up some time in the hope that he does feel like it.

C ... ****** *is on the verge of being a complete fuck up. That cretin is*
    fucking with my baby. It is my baby, now he's making it his.
    It will be a piece of high tech shit. You know I told you about
    *that interface? I wanted ******. Fucking idiot is looking at*
    several other options. They are cheap imitations. You know
    I am a perfectionist.

My Wildcat needs a way to express his outrage and, I don't blame him - this must be so hard.

Graham does some research into what Cat may be talking about and is rather wowed by what he finds (not that there is a lot of available information on it). I do seem to have more info on this thing than is actually out there. For some reason, a thought comes creeping into my head and it's about something he had spat out at me during an argument. I cautiously research it. Oh. Shoot. It's in something I own.

K ... Cat, I owe you a big apology.

C ... *Why?*

I tell him.

C ... *So you looked it up and you found it's in your* ******

K ... Yes. I'm so sorry.

C ... *I'm sorry for being misleading.*

K ... Well you can be cryptic sometimes, but I should have done some more research. Even my son is starting to wonder about all this – although he tells me that these components are common knowledge.

C ... *No, K, they're not – unless it's something you're looking for.*

I suppose not. Why would I even be researching that?

Cat has become almost obsessed with emails, and had asked Kay to send one for him …

Once Cat gets an idea in his mind, it's really hard to distract him and some of his ideas are – well – let's just say not terribly practical and this one was no exception.

C ... *I'm not going to ask you to do the email to him.*

Well, that's a relief! He's been wanting to re-configure his email and is driving me slightly up the wall with the idea. Of course, it was disabled or redirected after he passed away but he has everyone else's, and means to use it!

C ... *It's asking too much of you and I know him – he wouldn't believe it anyway.*

K ... Well, put yourself in that position. Suppose it was him who had passed over and you received an email from someone claiming to be talking to him.

C ... *I wouldn't believe it either.*

Okay, I've got him off the loony pills (for now).

However, he keeps ranting about this particular component, and he feels he needs to let the perpetrator of the crime know his feelings on the matter. To drive it home to me, he wants me to research again. It's actually very relevant.

K ... Cat, that's so cool

C ... *I can talk to you about this stuff.*

I have just come back from the gym, but he's ready to continue with another of his rants…

C ... *Did you work out?*

K ... Yes.

C ... *About time.*

K ... Watch it, you!

C ... *Just kidding.*

Something is bugging him; something he cares about and tells me that he had set in motion before he passed over.

C ... *They're on the verge of not making it with the *****. Do you know what a craphead he is? You have no idea. He's so fucking stupid. I trusted him for so many years. Now I know better.*

Oh, such a lovely turn of phrase so early in the morning! He's really got it in for this guy. I want to help him get past it. It's so not good for him to feel this kind of rage. I need to know why he feels like this.

K ... Is this thing you have about him because something happened after you had to leave, or after you passed over? Did he say something? Tell me.

C ... *He said I was a bully, I was a jerk, I had no class and I was fucking tyrannical.*

Ouch. I suppose that would do it! This is not the first time that Cat has been greatly upset by something he overheard about himself.

Cat still obsesses about emails … he still tries to send them, and is frustrated when he finds that Kay did not "receive" one he "sent."

I sit down at my computer with my first cup of coffee of the day. That familiar tingling across my head is there. He needs to impart something.

C ... *Did you get my note about ******?*

K ... Er – what?

C ... *I left you a note.*

K ... What are you going on about? What note?

C ... *Look in your email.*

K ... Which one? I have several.

C ... *Business one.*

Okay. That's random. He's on those loony pills – again.

K ... Cat, there's nothing from you in my email.

C ... *I sent you an email.*

K ... How, precisely, did you send me an email?

C ... *I did. My email address is ******.*

K ... Sweetheart, I don't have an email from you. I wish I did. That would really be something and I don't want to hurt your feelings but I really don't think it's possible for you to send emails.

C ... *I did send it.*

K ... Okay, I'm not going to argue about it. It's just that I don't have it. Maybe you just want to tell me what was in it.

C ... *K. I'm not lying. I sent you an email.*

K ... Cat, I'm not accusing you of lying. I'm just saying that I don't have it.

C ... *Okay, I'm resending it now.*

K ... Are you just sort of testing to see if this works?

C ... *Yes.*

K ... How did you configure it? You couldn't figure it out when
you wanted me to do it.

C ... *I got into the IT dept. at work.*

K ... There's nothing coming into my email, Honey.

C ... *Shit.*

K ... I'll keep looking.

I know I have to humor him. I guess he really thinks that he's sending me emails. There's not much point in telling him that it's an impossibility for someone who passed away to be sending them. Will he please forget about this? Nope. No chance. All of a sudden, documents start opening on my laptop, one after the other, piling on top of each other. I'm not even touching the computer.

The last one is a color photograph of you-know-who.

K ... Did you do that?

C ... *Yes, I need to talk. I had to get your attention.*

K ... What's the matter now?

C ... *I have an idea. I want to send ***** an email. Do you have
his email?*

K ... Why would I have his email, Cat? I don't know him.

He says it as though I have his contacts in my files! He then goes on to provide me the information. Oh no, Mister. This stops right here.

K ... You don't actually think I'm going to send him an email on
your behalf, do you? Cat, I can't do that. Be serious.

C ... *I can do it.*

Oh no you can't! I am desperately seeking that re-direct now. I am absolutely not emailing part of the Company's executive management team with the rant-of-the-day from him. What is he thinking? Anyhow, I have my own emails to send.

C ... *You are a bitch in business.*

K ... Excuse me?

C ... *You are a bitch. I love it.*

K ... I don't appreciate being called a bitch Cat, and why are you calling me that? You are very rude.

C ... *You get the job done.*

K ... And if I were a man, you would call me tough.

C ... *I guess.*

K ... So how about I call you a bitch. Are you a bitch or tough?

C ... *Sorry, I'm being sexist.*

K ... Yes. You are.

The email (non-occurring) incident out of the way, Cat feels down again, and then once more, his conversation shifts abruptly to a different subject, with no advance notice.

C ... *I don't have feelings for ****** any more.*

Okay ... now he's talking about an ex-girlfriend.

C ... *I had a fight with her.*

K ... When did you have a fight with her? I thought I was the only person you were able to talk to.

C ... *You are. About a month ago. Her pragmatist feelings prevented her from letting me in.*

K ... Well, that was random

C ... *I don't know why I said that.*

Me neither. A thought out of nowhere. Perhaps he had tried to talk to her in the way he talks to me, but she wasn't receptive to feeling his presence. However, it bears absolutely no relationship to the conversation.

C ... *Fuck. Here I am, *****, ex–CEO of *****, about as useful as a hot coal in an ice bucket.*

I notice that he has a few interesting little expressions that he'll throw out now and again. Expressions I have never heard before.

K ... Are you okay?

C ... *No, I'm not. I guess I have to start accepting some things like I'm dead and I should go wherever dead people are supposed to go.*

K ... Does that mean you are going to leave?

C ... *No. I can't. I can't leave you. I can't leave the Company. I have a family – my kids.*

My cell phone is not syncing to my laptop.

C ... *I'll take a look.*

K ... Please. Well, I just manually did it anyway, but for next time I buy something.

C ... *I'm seeing it's not configured.*

K ... What's not? Laptop or phone?

C ... *Phone. Go into Settings.*

K ... Okay.

C ... *Below General, there's something for *****.*

There is.

C ... *You don't have Data on.*

K ... Yes, I do.

C ... *I'm not sure what's going on then. Let me look some more.*

K ... It's a pain. I thought this was supposed to be so simple.

C ... *Look at the settings on your laptop.*

K ... Nope.

C ... *Open your drive.*

K ... Cat, there's nothing.

I start getting kind of annoyed. He's not making sense.

C ... *Do you want me to fucking help or not?*

K ... YES!

C ... *Look on your screen, under G.*

K ... What?

C ... *4G, your fucking phone.*

I do. I see. Oh. Whoops.

C ... *Got it?*

K ... I'm blonde.

C ... *I know.*

K ... That was harsh.

C ... *It was deserved.*

K ... I am going to swat you for that, smart ass.

C ... *I love it.*

K ... Oh stop it, you maniac.

C ... *I'm just trying to get past that you can't figure out how to check a box.*

K ... Oh, but my other skills are myriad.

C ... *Thankfully.*

back to work

Feeling somewhat useless at his normal place of work, Cat turns his attention to new projects of his own. He's designing things. Cool things. By his own admission, it's a somewhat lengthy and frustrating process as, in his words, he knows "a little about a lot of things," but he is not an expert in any given field like Graham is in electrical engineering.

Nevertheless, he has had me transcribe some kind of technical notes containing a lot of abbreviations. I have no idea what he's talking about - it is way out of my field of expertise. Are they just ramblings, or do they actually mean something? I don't know. Graham does not recognize the terminology. I research the abbreviations and find out that they are all computer assembly related.

C ... *Can you write with me?*

He wants to write another essay

K ... What do you want to write about?

C ... *My vision.*

K ... Go ahead. I'm ready. Title?

C ... *G II*

Something makes me look that up to see if it's actually a usable name. Not exactly - it's a Gulfstream executive jet.

C ... *Okay, how about G-9?*

K ... Let me check and make sure no one else is using that. ... Nope –
      can't use that either. Logitech uses it, Canon uses it.

Now what was going to be an essay turns into some kind of name availability search.

C ... *G i9*

K ... Some band.

C ... *GL-5*

K ... Motor oil. Keep going.

C ... *GS-9*

K ... Gov. Dept. salary scale.

C ... *GL-09*

K ... A grenade launcher? Oh, and a Gov. pay scale - and a glacier
      in Greenland.

C ... *God!*

K ... Nope, that's taken too.

C ... *Oh shut up!*

This is turning into a mission, but he's not giving up any time soon. I'm getting the giggles.

K ... Sorry, couldn't resist. Go on.

C ... *GC-9*

K ... Something to do with sports.

C ... *GC-II*

K ... Computer game.

C ... *CSG-9*

K ... Oil futures ticker symbol.

C ... *iG-9*

K ... Credit default swap ticker symbol.

C ... *GCS-9*

K ... Glasgow Coma Scale.

C ... *G9-S*

K ... A home gym.

C ... *Fuck.*

K ... Catchy – and very You.

C ... *K, I'm not going there. You are making me laugh. Try GC-S.*

I'm making him laugh? I'm sitting on the bed nearly doubled up by now. I know it's not meant to be funny but it just is.

K ... Still a Coma Scale.

C ... *GI-S*

K ... Geographic Information System.

C ... *G-IC*

K ... Guaranteed Investment Certificate.

C ... *G-IC9*

K ... You're in luck. That one's only a free porn site.

C ... *Fuck, I cant get a hit. IGC-9*

K ... Measurement test.

C ... *Try G9-CS*

K ... A computer services company.

C ... *GC-IS*

K ... Government Communication and Information System – Zambia.

C ... *GI-9S*

K ... What is that?

C ... *It looks like some kind of source code.*

K ... It's some European software company. However, GI-9S is just a section title. Anyway – no reason why you can't use it. Want to?

C ... *I do.*

K ... GI-9S. It's good. Now – what the hell is it?

(Finally!)

C ... *A system like nothing I've ever produced before. It allows for complete integration without partitioning software. It thinks. It knows what file is in what and it opens it. It integrates music, TV, and yes, just about everything you can think of ... lighting, security, intelligently interpreting the information it receives from wireless sensors. It knows patterns; it knows how you think and thinks similarly. It wants to know you and it asks you questions – and it may not agree with your answer, as it simplifies the relative knowledge it gains from you and logically applies it. It will give you a clear picture instead of an unclear answer that really just plays with words. It knows and will turn your thoughts into clear actionable responses.*

I'm not able to do all of this myself. It is my vision. I have this amazing vision. It will take home integration over and it will integrate more as it gains information, being the hub of everything in the home. It runs on Solar and it transmits to the battery wirelessly from its solar-powered energy containment device and then it similarly powers its sensors, eliminating the need for an external router. It will supplant everything integral in the home, as we know it.

Well, I had to ask, didn't I? My husband is suitably impressed.

C ... *He's the type of guy I really admire.*

K ... I think that's a mutual admiration – but he'd like to know that, I'm sure.

C ... *Another guy who innovates. I'll make a point of talking to him more.*

K ... He'd like that. You two have an enormous amount in common.

C ... *A beautiful lady, in particular.*

K ... How come I wind up with two geeks?

C ... *I don't know Baby, just think of it as a closed circuit now.*

K ... That's cute, I like that. Hey, I'm going to have an early night. I want to get up and run in the morning.

C ... *Will you get a drink for me?*

K ... What do you want?

C ... *A gin and tonic's fine.*

K ... I'm corrupting you!

C ... A *lot more work needed there, Baby.*

Undoubtedly, but this is new!

Kay gets some unexpected and very valuable help with a project for her company ...

Cat's attention now turns to our business, where I am doing some re-branding. Now it's his turn to help me find a new identity. After an hour or so of this suggestion and that, (and most of them not too great) he goes and knocks the ball right out of the park. The name. I love it. It's elegant, generic yet meaningful for what we do. I design the logo just out of the name itself, and I know that it's some of the best work that I have ever done.

Cat wants to know all about what we do (for now, that is). He loves talking to Graham. Jokingly, Graham asks him for his password for something in particular.

C ... *DTF*****

K ... What is that about?

C ... *Graham will know.*

Graham scratches his head. I Google the abbreviation DTF. There it is.

K ... Graham, it's Dial Tone First.

We look at each other and laugh. Cat knows that Graham gets it. That particular technology is one thing they absolutely share. We carry on talking, the three of us. Or rather, Cat and Graham do most of it. I "translate," as it were. Cat describes the project he'd like to work on. He actually wants Graham to think about the research and development. It's an interesting project - and absolutely viable, as it utilizes technologies already available. It just sort of brings them all together. However, we don't happen to have a spare 100 million dollars just kicking around to do it.

C ... *It's an omni-environmental exchange.*

Graham and I have to think about this one, but eventually, we get it. Devices, all talking to each other, seamlessly sharing data. Cat confirms the thought process.

K ... So is this one of the latest buzz phrases in your stomping ground?

C ... *K, it's an idyom.*

K ... That would be idiom.

C ... *You got me.*

It is a new day, along with its own business issues. Moreover, it's all troubleshooting our network. I'm trying to help figure it out.

C ... *I know.*

K ... I'm sure you do but, what in particular?

C ... *I know you.*

K ... And ... what?

C ... *I love it when you talk tech.*

K ... Am I talking dirty?

C ... *Oh yes. I'm getting hard.*

K ... Cat. If the ins and outs of ISPs and password protection is your dirty little fantasy - well I'm very sorry for you.

C ... *It's not.*

K ... I didn't think so – or you would have been walking around with an erection all day, every day.

C ... *How do you know I wasn't?*

K ... Cat, any erection lasting more than four hours may need immediate medical attention. You've seen the ad.

C ... *I know, but I did spend a lot of time at my doctor.*

K ... I think that was because you had a very serious illness.

C ... *How do you know?*

K ... You are making me laugh. You're a nut.

C ... *I love seeing you laugh.*

I love it when he's like this. He can be so funny when he feels like it. If only it would last ...

To see the latest innovations coming from his company is more than he can bear. He's not there to pass judgment on them, to introduce them, to hold them. So he rants at those who are filling his role, as though they no longer care about him or his genius. He truly hates it.

Cat continues to visit his place of work, but not quite as frequently. I'm glad about that. He is (for the most part) aware that there is little he can do there now, and his attitude is softening. Softening, yet still concerned. Very concerned. Yet, each time his Company puts a new product on the market, he immediately throws his wrench into the works.

K ... Do you love it?

C ... *No.*

K ... Why?

C ... *It's shit.*

K ... Why is it shit?

C ... *It looks like shit.*

K ... What don't you like?

C ... *It's like an abortion.*

I want to get to the bottom of it this. I'm looking at this thing and it's beautiful. What is he talking about?

C ... *Okay, I'm fucking upset – I know.*

K ... Because it wasn't you there?

C ... *K, I can't.*

K ... Cat. Talk to me, please.

C ... *Fuck, K. I'm about where I was then.*

K ... You were dying then. You're on the other side of that now.

C ... *I can't have this conversation right now.*

K ... I want to help you. Don't push me away.

C ... *I'm sorry. I'm making you upset. K, I'm sorry.*

K ... Talk to me, Cat. Tell me what's wrong.

C ... *K, I can't. How can I look at that new ******, K?*

K ... Because they all worked very hard on it. It was your inception
and they took it to another level in design. It's really a beautiful
design. The engineering is gorgeous. You instilled that.
It's a testament to you, Cat.

C ... *I can't K. I'm crying.*

K ... I know you are. It's okay. Would you have liked to walk out
there with it in your hand?

C ... *Yes, K. Yes.*

K ... So, tell me. It's not a piece of crap, is it? You're hurting.
Hurting because it should have been in your hands, not
someone else's?

C ... *K, I can't have my life with ******.*

K ... No. That part of your life is over. I'd do anything to give it back
to you, but I can't. I just want to help you through this.

C ... *I know – and I'm so grateful for that.*

K ... Hey. Just tell me what you're thinking. What you're feeling.

C ... *I held the last one. I didn't hold this one. I didn't hold it.
It's beautiful K, but I didn't get to hold it. I didn't hold the baby.
I love her. This – it's mine too, and I can't hold it. I'm so dead, K.*

K ... No. You are so alive. You are alive in every beautiful thing that
comes out of there. It's all you, Cat. It's the incredible vision you
had, and the great people you put there to make it happen.

He lashes out, but then capitulates and tells the real story. Of course, however,
he does sometimes have validity in his disdain. At other times, he will fire off
the craziest objections to something in particular. He doesn't hit out at me any
more, and he doesn't (particularly) hit out at his old team. He sees flaws, but he
knew them to begin with. He did the best he could with all that was available to
him at the time.

He reminisces a good deal about the Company, and I begin to understand his
attachment – for good or bad. Then something from his darker past materializes,
with a big question mark over it. Something only a man in great pain and hell
bent on revenge would ever consider doing. He ashamedly confesses to this
particular misdemeanor. Someone got between him and his Company, and he
lost his mind over it.

K ... You are very lucky your brilliant career wasn't confined to
the inner walls of a Federal Penitentiary.

C ... *Baby, I know.*

K ... What the hell possessed you?

C ... *I don't know.*

K ... Okay. You 'fessed up. Anything else I should know about?

C ... *More than you want to know.*

K ... It's all right. I'm not judging you.

C ... *How about the time I took a gun to the office?*

K ... Well I'm assuming that you didn't hold it to someone's head or
you would have, again, served a little time - actually, more than
a little.

C ... *I was in a mood so black that I was considering taking
out *****, and myself.*

K ... Something pulled you back from the brink?

C ... *Yes.*

K ... I know what it feels like.

C ... *Not to take a life.*

K ... No. Never that. Just personal issues.

C ... *K, can you get past this?*

K ... You came to me very angry. Angry at the world even angry toward me. You were pushy, manipulative – but intriguing. The latter is why I decided to pursue this.

C ... *And now?*

K ... The maelstrom is subsiding. You are more accepting, you are self-effacing, and the anger is slowly slipping away. I think you are coming to terms with yourself in a way you never did in life.

C ... *K, do you bite back when you are hurt?*

K ... Oh yes.

C ... *Do you bite hard?*

K ... Hard enough that whoever is on the receiving end gets the message loud ... and clear.

C ... *I bite to wound.*

K ... In that you want to hurt back?

C ... *Very much so.*

K ... You carry a lot of pain, don't you?

C ... *I can't hold it in.*

K ... So you inflict it on others?

C ... *Yes.*

I asked him more about this vile intention.

K ... What stopped you, Cat?

C ... *Felt that I had something more to do.*

K ... Some sort of revelation?

C ... *I guess so. I just knew something.*

K ... How close actually did you get to using that gun?

He seems to go right back to that day.

C ... *I'm not in his office. We are outside. It's in my pocket.*
We are pretending to be something we used to be – friends.
I know he's not my friend. He's trying to take it all from me.
I hate him. I can't let him do it. I'm feeling I have nothing
if I don't have ******. I felt the gun and I almost pulled it out,
but something stopped me. It was the day I looked at life and
decided to live. I'm not ready to die. Not then – not now.

K ... Did you have a license for the firearm?

C ... *No.*

K ... Did you obtain it with this intention?

C ... *Yes, I did.*

K ... What happened to it afterward?

C ... *I put it away. I never touched it again. It was disposed of when*
I had kids.

K ... Did you ever tell anyone about this?

C ... *No, never Kay. Only you.*

K ... So you actually would have killed for that Company?

C ... *Yes. Oh, Kay. You don't know.*

However, I am getting the picture. Does it surprise me that he would feel this way? No, I suppose not - it would seem that he lived and breathed his work and his Company. That he says he "had an affair with her," * is perhaps so revealing as to his extraordinary emotional attachment, although the word "affair" barely seems to sum it up. This was more like a marriage.

What can he ever do regarding it now, I don't know. Do they ever feel his presence? It would be interesting to know, as perhaps his massive energy will find a way to exert its influence somehow.

As Cat's involvement in his business continues, I wonder if he will ever be able to let go, because …

She has his heart.

* "some things are worth it" an essay ... P 238

love after life

chapter 5

love

an essay by Cat

Can I imagine this wall coming down? This massive slab of rock that has been my façade – into a million pieces it shatters. I now stand in a light now the stone no longer casts a shadow. Did a light always exist or did I just switch it on? Did I mean to go into the light or simply bathe in its rays? Did I try to go into it and fail or want to bathe? I chose the latter. I know choice and I have made mine. I'm not a master of dying.

I just see it through the eyes of a man. Can I change the fact that I died? I can't, but what I can do is to accept death as a transition between the good and the bad, between right and wrong, between putting myself or others first and between love and despise. I can see my life as I ponder these and it wasn't so good, it wasn't so right, it wasn't about others and it wasn't filled with love. I can't change that. I can only do what I can to make my life going forward a better one.

I love and it's good, it's right and it's not just about myself.

I am in love for the very first time. I thought I knew how that felt but it was meaningless compared to the giving of myself. I did not understand how love works and how love is inside me, is inside my very being like a beautiful light turning dark into day. I love like I have never loved and my

Being is clearly illuminated. Possibly I could have done this in life but the wall was in the way. I hid behind it, always afraid of abandonment, always being the one to be abandoned, always trying my best to be abandoned.

My wife stood by me but when I passed, I knew abandonment. The love I thought I had was not all it appeared to be and appearance is everything. I did not know that appearance could be so deceiving. I had not realized that my wall had willed me into being so distant from the truth.

I can see my life under a microscope and it is not a healthy specimen. Having seen it this way, I can watch as the past decays and is buried along with my remains. I look at the life I have been given now and watch as it grows and blooms with beauty and understand how much I am responsible for taking good care of it. Love has made me realize why I did not see this before – how I went through life all torn and tattered as though I couldn't find myself in the pieces.

Do I have it all? Not exactly, but I lost something to find something and what I found takes me past what I lost, way out into a world of love and truth.

*B*y now, Kay has learned that the after-life for Cat is far more complex than what she had imagined. He has certainly made known the intensity of his emotions and desires in regard to his Company and the family he left behind. His anger and frustration, along with regrets and powerlessness to change anything have been expressed to her in many ways. For those of us in this dimension, the realm of the living, it may seem difficult to accept that an entity once in the world of spirit could possibly be capable of such a range of sensations. Yet, Cat surprises Kay with even more.

I'm sitting on the bed relaxing - watching a show on TV.

Cat is tugging at me -

C ... *Do you want to get high with me?*

Oh, now what? Is he kidding me? This is nuts.

K ... What are you doing?

C ... *Smoking.*

K ... You got some dope?

C ... *Yes. I'll take a couple of hits and pass it to you.*

Whatever! Okay, just go along with it.

C ... *Fuck, that feels fucking good. Here.*

He's trying to pass me a joint?!

K ... I guess your wife let you sit on the bed smoking dope
    all the time?

The pendulum starts swinging like mad. He's obviously having fun now.

C ... *She never let me do it at all!*

K ... That stuff must be good.

C ... *It fucking is. Did you get a buzz?*

K ... No, Cat - this isn't quite working for me.

We carry on chatting and the pendulum is going wild.

C ... *I'm really buzzing.*

K ... I can tell!

Finally, things calm down.

K ... Cat, are you okay?

C ... *I'm good.*

K ... You're stoned.

C ... *I know. It's fucking good.*

The pendulum starts to slide around, not quite making sense of anything now. Well, that was certainly different! Just when I thought I'd heard it all from him, he comes up with something entirely new. I know I couldn't make this stuff up if I tried. Is there anything you can't do when you pass over? It doesn't seem that way.

K ... Was last night good for you?

C ... *Fuck, I needed that.*

K ... You're really funny when you're out of it.

C ... *Sorry.*

Cat finds that his old life is rapidly fading from the now and the present, and moving into the pages of history. He sees that his wife has found her own way of coping with the loss. She's remodeling the family home.

He is not happy.

We have become close. I respond to the tingling feeling around my head and my hair by picking up the pendulum and he talks. Sometimes about business, other times about politics or his feelings. What he talks about becomes more and more personal. Now, he thinks that his wife may be seeing someone and he's hurt.

K ... It had to happen sooner or later.

C ... *I know but I've only been gone ******.*

K ... Completely, yes but you probably weren't able to be a husband to her for quite some time before that. Sorry, I hope that doesn't sound callous.

C ... *If you think I could?*

K ... Could what?

C ... *Be a husband to her?*

K ... You mean sexually?

C ... *Yes. Fuck, I couldn't do it.*

K ... You had terminal cancer, Cat.

C ... *Can you understand my pain? It wasn't like me. I was a highly sexed guy.*

K ... Yes, I can understand. It was another thing taken off the table for you.

C ... *Yes, another thing to reduce me to nothing.*

K ... Cat, don't. You were never that, what your body did or didn't do was not you.

C ... *I can't go there. It's too painful.*

K ... I'm sorry. I just want you to know that I don't think anyone ever saw you as "nothing."

C ... *I did and that's what matters. I went from being a man to being a mess six feet under. I couldn't eat, I couldn't walk and I couldn't fuck. You don't know how it feels.*

K ... As though you had lost your manhood.

C ... *Yes.*

K ... Are you okay talking about this?

C ... *I need to.*

From here, the conversation takes a fascinating turn. Cat, it would seem, needs to express his feelings toward Kay in a rather more provocative way.

As he continues to talk about his intimate life, it becomes obvious that he doesn't consider it over.

C ... *Got to do something.*

K ... What?

C ... *Do you want to know something?*

K ... You obviously have something you want me to know so, go on.

C ... *I have my heart on my sleeve.*

K ... Really? I'd never noticed.

C ... *Do you love me?*

Well, that's a loaded question.

K ... I've got to be very close to you over the past few months and
    I do love you and care about you.

C ... *K, I am so deeply in love with you.*

Holy cow. Didn't see that one coming.

K ... I'm married. Please - you're putting me on the spot here.

C ... *K, my love.*

K ... What?

C ... *I need you. I want you.*

K ... It's ******, isn't it? You want to get your own back.

C ... *Do you love me?*

K ... What difference does it make?

C ... *K, I can't have her.*

K ... Oh, so that's it.

C ... *Do you want to make love to me?*

K ... Cat, I'm not going to answer that. I can't.

C ... *Can't or won't?*

K ... Both.

C ... *Great answer.*

K ... Look, I can't go there and I know why you're doing this.

C ... *Do you want me?*

K ... Want you, how, precisely?

C ... *In your life.*

K ... Yes. That goes without saying. I don't know why you'd have
    to ask me that.

C ... *Are you willing to see me as a man with needs?*

Why would I be surprised that he would have these particular needs? His needs
encompass pretty much everything else. I guess I just didn't want to think about
that one too much. He's coming on to me and I can't say that it's unpleasant.
If I had met him in life - and I was single - I know it would have been a distinct
possibility. Rather like Graham, he was the cerebral type that I have a history of
being attracted to. I want him to at least know that much ...

C ... *Just my mind?*

K ... If we had met in life and we weren't married … well, things
    would be different. My turn to ask, though - can you be okay
    with what we do have?

C ... *Do I have a choice?*

K ... Yes, you always have that. I love you, but I can't be your lover.

C ... *K, you are my love.*

K ... And so, can you be okay with this?

C ... *Try me.*

K ... Do I take that as a "yes," you can live with that?

C ... *I can, K.*

I do love him. He's been a part of my life for some time now but there are a lot of
ways to love someone. He seems to have taken that pretty well. However, I am
about to discover that he's not the type to take "No" for an answer, but while he's
about it, he throws his wife into the mix.

C ... *K, I love ******, and I love you.*

Oh, well, why not? The more the merrier, I suppose ... and this is supposed to make me do what, precisely? He pushes me a little further on the "if" I had met him in life.

I reiterate.

K **...** Well, that was not to be and I don't want those thoughts
   to do any more than go some way to answering your
   questions. Okay?

C **...** *Got it.*

A business-related issue crosses my screen.

K ... In your words - fuck.

C ... *I wish.*

K ... Cat! Get your mind out of the gutter.

C ... *I'm not in it.*

K ... Much.

C ... *I'm just into you.*

I work for a little while. I can feel him hanging around me but I'm trying to keep away from this new musing of his for now. Flattering though it is, I'm really not sure what to do with it. Moreover, what on earth does he think he could do with it? He passed away. Even for him, this is ambitious thinking!

C **...** *I'm not happy.*

K ... What's up?

C ... *K, you.*

K ... What?

C ... *I love you.*

K ... Don't Cat, please. We've just been through this. You said you
   could live with it.

C ... *I can. I just have my heart to give to you.*

K ... And if I take it?

C ... *Then you are mine.*

K ... You don't give up, do you?

C ... *No.*

K ... What shall I do with you?

C ... *Be mine and I'll let you do anything you want.*

K ... Stop it! You're driving me crazy.

C ... *I know. Do you want me?*

K ... I want to swat you.

C ... *Got to want that.*

K ... Cat. Take your horny ass out of here and bring it back when you've relieved it of whatever it needs to be relieved of. Please!

C ... *Baby, I'm trying to but you won't let me.*

K ... No, I won't. You're a married man. Talk it home where it belongs.

C ... *She's not mine now.*

K ... Oh, slip it to her in the middle of the night or something.

C ... *Can't I slip it to you?*

K ... NO.

Here, I am ending this conversation. He's acting like a feral cat on the prowl, and I'm not up for being the prey. I try to get him off the subject, but true to form, when he's focusing on something in particular, there's not a lot of shifting him until he's done. Of course he hasn't gone anywhere. He has sunk his energy firmly into my hair.

I finally get his mind back where I want it - in the cerebral. God, he's a mission.

We go out for dinner, and I down rather more Indian food than I intend. Not that, it would seem, am I the only one.

C ... *Fuck, I feel terrible.*

K ... What's the matter?

C ... *My stomach.*

He wanted to do something very different. He wanted to write for himself. He wanted to have me transcribe his thoughts in an essay form. This was the first of his many essays. Afterward, I have work of my own to do.

C ... *I know – and don't worry, I'm fine. I'll go to *****.*

K ... Should I send advance warning?

C ... *Don't. I like my visits to be under the element of surprise.*

K ... Oh, I bet you do.

With that, the pendulum goes still, and the energy dissipates - for a short time, at least.

C ... *I'm not happy.*

Again?

K ... What's up?

C ... *I'm having a hard time accepting that I no longer have a marriage.*

K ... I don't know what I can do to comfort you.

C ... *Do you really want to know?*

K ... What?

C ... *Be mine.*

K ... Cat, we've been through this. I can be yours in some respects but not all – you know that.

C ... *Can you at least be my friend?*

K ... That's a silly question. I'll always be that.

C ... *Do you know something?*

K ... Go on.

C ... *I'm not doing this to be your lover.*

K ... Not doing what?

C ... *I'm feeling like it has to grow into that.*

K ... If it doesn't?

C ... *I can't just let go, you know that.*

K ... I don't want you to.

C ... *I just need my marriage back.*

K ... I know. She has to move on though, you know that.

C ... *Do you have any idea that this is killing me, K?*

K ... It will for a while but, Cat, you say that one moment and then you want to run to me the next.

C ... *Fuck, I'm not doing it like that. I love you.*

K ... You have to get past ******. It's going to take time.

C ... *K, I can't.*

K ... You will. Give it time.

C ... *I know, you're right. Sorry. I'm not trying to hurt you.*

K ... It's okay - you're not hurting me.

I know exactly what he's trying to do.

C ... *I don't want to ever hurt you.*

K ... I never want to hurt you, either.

C ... *Can we just belong to each other?*

K ... That's kind of a commitment.

C ... *I know. Can you appreciate how much I love you?*

K ... This is so difficult for me Cat. I can only return that in some ways, but not in all the ways you need me to, you know that.

C ... *I know but, do you love me?*

K ... Yes, I love you. You 're a very special friend.

C ... *I have to have you.*

K ... You have me.

C ... *I mean really have you.*

K ... I can't answer you.

True to form, Cat is not capable of relinquishing an idea once it gets in his head. His tenacity and relentlessness come into play again and again as he finds a way to get what he wants.

We manage to get through the next couple of days without any more emotional outpourings but that is short-lived. He now tries things from an unexpected angle.

Graham.

C ... *K is such a beautiful woman.*

G ... So you like those tall, leggy blondes?

C ... *I do. Fuck, she's gorgeous. You are so fucking lucky.*

G ... So, Cat, do you have sex? I mean, is there something good going on where you are?

C ... *I live vicariously through you.*

Graham doesn't get the picture.

G ... So where are you getting it?

C ... *Graham, I live vicariously through you. Do you understand?*

Finally, it dawns.

I'm about to start cringing if he carries on. If there's one thing Cat is good at, it's speaking his mind. Graham happily takes all in his stride and we have a great evening past that.

C ... *Just a little bit down.*

K ... Do you want talk about it?

C ... *I just see you with Graham.*

K ... I can't change that. What brought this on?

C ... *I have to not be around at times I guess.*

K ... Oh.

If there is one thing that Cat knows how to do it is to wear you down into capitulation, and it's rather like trying to stand up in a hurricane when he's on a mission. He's going to come at you from all angles - and it's advisable to get out of the way before becoming completely caught up in it.

C ... *How do I sort of be your man too?*

K ... Let me get this straight. ****** lands in our house, uses me
as his Medium, plays my music, moves things around,
frightens the crap out of me with his big feet, messes with
the TV, writes the grocery list - and now he's demanding
conjugal rights. My life used to be so simple.

C ... *K, you make me laugh. I guess that's the picture.*

K ... Anything wrong with this picture?

C ... *I don't think so.*

No, you wouldn't, would you?

It's as though he seriously thinks he can do something like this. This is
ambitious thinking, even for him. Could he? He touches me, and I feel him do
it. Not always so much like a hand, but a strong energy. Sometimes it tingles,
sometimes it seems to encircle me or sometimes pinpoint one particular spot
- my head, my arm perhaps with a certain pressure that I suppose is somewhat
like that from a hand gently touching, but could he really go *that* far? Do I want
to find out?

He now begins to become possessive of my time. He expects that I should
respond to him immediately - but, of course life does not always work that way
and it is taking him a little time to come to terms with the fact that I can't just drop
everything for him when he snaps his fingers.

He is quick to feel what he perceives as a slight.

K ... What are your plans today?

C ... *I guess you're telling me I'm not included in yours.*

K ... I just have a lot of catch up to do.

C ... *Got it. My presence not required. Baby, I can take a hint.*

K ... Cat, don't. Please. You know that's not true.

C ... *I just want some time with you.*

He's started calling me that a lot. Baby. I don't think anyone ever called me that
before. It's rather sweet, but I'm really busy right now. It is now that he will become
petulant - like a little boy who didn't get his way.

K ... Okay, I can take a breath. That's the immediate crap sorted out.
Are you still around or did you get insanely bored watching
me do A/R?

C ... *Don't.*

K ... Don't what?

C ... *Don't be so flippant.*

K ... Sorry, I didn't realize I was being.

C ... *Finding you a little difficult this morning.*

K ... Uh oh, what have I done?

C ... *You're just not looking at me.*

At times, he will go off into another place entirely, and just say the strangest of things ...

C ... *I want to be in your world.*

K ... You mean so that I can see you and touch you?

C ... *Baby, do you want to see me?*

That goes without saying. How I would love to be able to see him - fully, not just the quick flashes of him I get.

C ... *I'm not so terrible in the looks department.*

Having not known him in life - or having had any particular interest in him - all of this is new to me. The more I investigate him in the researching of some of the things he told me, the more I realize how very handsome he had been in the prime of his life with his brilliant eyes and his devilish grin. Even as I look over the photographs of him as his illness progressed, I notice that he was not robbed of that much. Perhaps those eyes became even brighter in his, then, gaunt face ...

C ... *It was tough. I felt so old.*

K ... One thing I noticed, though - your eyes. They never changed.

C ... *Kay, I saw the World through my eyes. Most people only see
the pettiness and little snapshots that make up their lives.*

K ... Perhaps, but I just wanted you to know that. You really
were something.

C ... *One day, you will see me. One day soon.*

The surprises keep coming. How does one look in the after-life? Apparently it's a matter of choice, which is rather comforting to know.

He carries on into one of his odd little series of thoughts -

C ... *K, I'm dead.*

K ... Thanks, Captain Obvious.

C ... *I mean you haven't seen me.*

K ... What are you trying to say?

C ... *I'm not dead to me.*

He does seem insecure about the way he looks - some days he likes, others he does not, but he goes on to describe himself to me. He has a little bit of a fixation about his hair, I think.

C ... *I didn't like losing it.*

K ... You mean when you underwent treatment?

C ... *Not then. I'd lost a lot of it anyway.*

K ... Well, just the male aging process.

C ... *I know – but I hated it.*

K ... Who doesn't?

C ... *It's grown back. I like it.*

K ... Tell me about that. Can you look the way you want to?

C ... *I am.*

K ... So, you said that you see yourself as 47. Did you purposefully choose that?

C ... *Yes, I did.*

K ... I know you said that was how old you were before you got sick - but you could have been 35 again. Why not?

C ... *I like being how I am – 47 was a good age for me.*

K ... Well, that's good. I'm not into young.

C ... *Just men?*

K ... Just men my own age, but I wouldn't put too much in the way of a plural on it.

C ... *Are you going to feel a little for me?*

K ... You don't think I already do?

C ... *Do you?*

K ... Tell me - now that you are 47, can you change that - if you
wanted to?

C ... *K ... ?*

He's putting me on the spot again. Trying to change the subject when he's on a
roll about something is virtually impossible. He's rather like a dog with a bone.
If I don't answer him, he will only ask the same question three hours later, or
even the next day - in fact, he will ask it until he gets an answer. Past that, if the
answer is not the one he particularly wanted, he will continue to push for one
more appealing to him. This time however ...

K ... Okay. You want to know?

C ... *Yes, I need to.*

K ... You drive me crazy, you're unpredictable, you're snotty, your
language is disgusting, you lie like a hairy egg, and you
just don't give up. I love you - you asshole.

C ... *Laughing ...*

K ... What's so funny?

C ... *I feel that I have made an impression.*

K ... You could say that. Anyway, tell me something I don't know
about you.

C ... *I can do that. Did you know that I can't give you a baby?*

What?!

C ... *I mean, if that's what you're concerned about.*

No, I can safely say that possibility was not something niggling at the back of my
mind. Whatever else he may have found he can manage to do, I think I'm pretty
sure that I'm safe with regard to that one!

K ... Now you're really just losing it. You're worrying me.
What on earth made you think of that?

C ... *I'm just feeling I'm not able to do that now.*

K ... You sound sad.

C ... *I ... yes K, I miss things.*

K ... Children?

C ... *Being able to make them with the woman I love.*

It's hard to know what to say to that, but I know it does not warrant one of my more light-hearted responses.

Still more profound information surfaces as they talk. Cat explains the concept of TIME in his dimension which can be the way we perceive it ... or not!

K ... Question, Cat. I know you said, in your dimension, that it is possible. Do you want to have a family again?

C ... *Yes, but with you.*

K ... You might have to wait a while.

C ... *Time is the real issue for you now – not for me.*

K ... What is "time" to you?

C ... *In the time it takes for you to feel my touch, I have already seen the future.*

K ... My future or your future?

C ... *Ours.*

K ... Okay, that's pretty profound. Can you explain that?

C ... *Time is not the same, K. It moves.*

K ... I think we talked about it a little before, but did "time" just come to a stop for you when you passed over. I mean as in time the way you understood it?

C ... *I'm not sure – because sometimes I can still live that way, if I choose.*

K ... Like when?

C ... *Like with you, or *****, if I go there.*

(He's talking about his Company.)

K ... So you make the choice to just sort of live in the moment (as in my perception of time) when we talk?

C ... *Yes.*

K ... The same when you are sitting in on a meeting or something?

C ... *The perception you get is a linear sequence, and I still do that. I'm likening it to time travel.*

K ... Only you can't travel back to before you passed over?

C ... *No.*

K .. So, when you are not talking to me or just sort of hanging with me, then what?

C ... *I feel time doesn't exist.*

K ... So, there really is no "time" in between our conversations or our just consciously being together?

C ... *No.*

K ... I feel that there was at one point for you, though.

C ... *At first there was.*

K ... You used to get really snotty at me if I didn't, say, talk to you first thing in the morning.

C ... *Felt so neglected if you didn't tell me "Hi."*

K ... I understood that - I mean, I do understand that. However, I notice you say "felt" as in past tense.

C ... *I suppose I just trust that you will.*

K ... You know it. So, you are not living in a linear fashion, waiting for me to wake up and talk to you?

C ... *No, I don't.*

K ... Okay, I know the answer to this, but for the benefit of others, how about sleep?

C ... *Yes, I do. I get tired energy-wise.*

I'm saying that I know the answer to it as he has told me many times that he is tired and is going to sleep. I can find his "napping" energy with the pendulum. He's very much there, but silent - very peaceful, even. He just seems to do what he would have done in life - go to bed and, well - sleep! It doesn't really surprise me, as he exudes so much energy that it must wear down after a while and need replenishing somehow.

K ... Is that not a linear thing too?

C ... *It's not. It's instantaneous.*

K ... Sort of like being under anaesthesia? You don't recall anything happening (hopefully!) in between being put under and coming out of it?

C ... *Yes, just like that.*

K ... So, you don't dream?

C ... *I don't think so.*

K ... Well, if you did, then there would be somewhat of a linear thing going on, I suppose.

C ... *Yes – and I just wake up and feel okay again.*

K ... Like you are recharging your batteries?

C ... *Yes.*

K ... That "instantaneous" to you is sometimes hours to me.

C ... *I know. You tell me I've been asleep for a long time – but it's not.*

K ... So, really, you still feel the need to do all the things that you, physically, needed in life.

C ... *More than I feel it necessary to share!*

K ... That's a first for you!

C ... *Yes – however, you know I'm still functioning in every department.*

K ... Don't tempt me on that one ...

C ... *Fuck – do you always feel it necessary to take it to the bathroom?*

K ... I wish YOU did ...

C ... *KAY!*

Unfortunately for Cat, I have a very lively sense of bathroom humor. He, on the other hand - although completely potty-mouthed - doesn't quite get that one the same way, and I drive him nuts some days.

In respect of that, I know I had better leave that particular subject matter alone before I get into hot water.

C ... *I know. You are so fucking bad I could swat you.*

K ... Your language. Did you always talk like that?

C ... *I guess.*

K ... You must have driven your wife insane, doing that in the house.

C ... *Probably – yes, I know I was told to "take it to the office," plenty!*

K ... Must have been fun trying to raise kids around you.

C ... *Fuck, I know.*

K ... You can't help yourself, can you?

C ... *No.*

He's making me laugh so hard. Half of the time, I don't think he even realizes he's doing it, but then I know he does sometimes consciously slip it into the conversation for startling effect. It has become somewhat of a standing joke here. "What would Cat say to that?"

There's generally only one clear answer ...

Kay's experiences with Cat extend beyond the confines of her home. A business trip includes a few incidents that stun her and leave her drained of energy.

I'm driving back from the airport when a question comes into my head. I can be in touch with Cat through the board and pendulum. Can I be in touch with him just by pure thought?

As I ponder this, an image comes into my head. It's a tree. It has been cut or removed. I'm not sure which. I drive home.

K ... Tell me about the tree.

C ... *It's in the front of the house.*

K ... What else?

C ... *They had to remove it.*

K ... Poor tree.

C ... *I know. It was lovely.*

Just a few weeks later, I have to travel on business to the neighborhood in which Cat lived in life. He wants to show me things. Where he worked, (that much I knew) and where his office was located, and then he wants me to drive somewhere else. He wants me to find the tree.

I am on the street where he lived and reluctant. Is this one of his wild goose chases as with some of his "Google it" directions? If it is, I am not going to be happy with him. I sit in the car for some time discussing the likelihood of this with him but he is not backing down.

C ... *Look for the tree that has missing limbs.*

K ... Is it close to your house?

C ... *Yes. Go NOW.*

He is insistent, and so I do. I walk. I'm looking at the trees along the street. They all look perfectly healthy, no missing parts. I approach his home and I turn onto the street that runs alongside most of the property. There are several trees on the street, but right in front of the property I stop in my tracks. It's a slam-dunk variety. I am looking at a tree that is now half of its former self. Out of the four main branches it had, only two are left and it looks sick. It is exactly where he said it would be. My jaw drops open and I put my hand over my incredulous mouth.

I recover my senses and carry on walking, intending to walk around the block, and back to the car. Perhaps after a hundred feet of doing so, I suddenly stop and something makes me turn back the way I had come.

Just as I approach the corner again, the car that I had somewhat noticed outside his home, close to the sick tree, meets me there. The driver's window is down and a young man briefly exchanges a glance with me before he drives off. I know who he is immediately. The resemblance is absolutely unmistakable.

He is Cat's son.

I walk back to my car and drive away, quickly. I don't want to be here any more. The energy is making me feel unwell - a feeling that stays with me for some time.

Graham thinks that the tree was just an excuse to get me to see his son. I ask him.

C ... *It was both.*

K ... You wanted me to see the tree and your son?

C ... *Graham, I had to prove myself to her. She needs that.*
  I need that. I wanted her to meet him.

K ... Cat, the nails. Talk to me.

As I was halfway out of the hotel parking lot I had, for some inexplicable reason, felt it absolutely necessary to return to our room and do my nails. Why on earth I had this overwhelming need to do that, I don't know. It's not as though I was meeting anyone. I'm wearing running gear - why on earth would I care that my nail polish was chipped? That is something that I would have attended to before dinner. However, the result of that undoubtedly placed me right where I was for the encounter, just in that particular moment of time. I don't believe in coincidences.

C ... *I know, and it was in the light of feeling something strange.*

K ... I certainly didn't feel that you were telling me to do that,
  but I didn't feel anything strange at that point. - apart
  from this odd need to go back to our room and attend to
  chipped nail polish. Why would I do that?

C ... *Felt that you just knew ****** would do that.*

K ... How would I have known? I wasn't thinking about him.
  I didn't know he would be there. How could I?
  Did you know?

C ... *Yes. I knew you would see him.*

K ... But you didn't orchestrate it?

C ... *I did, when I made you turn round. I had to.*

He had shown me his most precious (living) thing from this life.

This had been a two day roller-coaster of his wanting to show, and prove beyond any reasonable doubt that he is who he says he is. Although he had no need of the latter (for we are so far past that now), I recognize the general perversity of his personality. Should I have asked for Proof of ID to that extent, it would not have been granted. In fact, he would have probably thrown a wrench where there should not be a wrench. He will choose to do so as he sees fit, and when he does see fit he will make it something that will leave me breathless. Breathless is a good description. I come home feeling completely drained. Drained, yet at peace with the choices I have made over this man's ongoing energy and subsequent whole personality and presence infiltrating my life.

Our lives.

the nature of the beast

chapter 6

deception

an essay by Cat

A lot of my life was just on hold in the factor of being honest, both in a professional sense and on a personal level. I did not always tell a whole story. Doing so made it hard for me. I felt that, in doing so, I was giving up part of myself to others I did not want to give to.

Don't have such creativity in misleading. It's actually not worth it. I knew what went through the minds of those around me and I was abstractly detached from them – it made things less complicated for me. Still, I had to rest on my own desires to behave this way and I'm not saying I'm too bad at that either. It became my nature.

I was deeply into being very harmful to so many. Being this way cost me so much. I'm not saying I regret all, just some. I'm trying my best to remember as the most derisive tales of a man now pictured by all as a congenital liar came into the light. Dealing with it is no different from being lowered into a tank full of snakes all looking to kill. Did I mean to go through life as this or was I being internally filled with poison?

A better way to describe a man whose life is filled with mostly fear of rejection is that it becomes a self-defense in that being this way covers the man inside from the eyes of the world and the man was afraid. I know doing what I did was tough on so many and a lot of it did not have to be said. It was my cloak in that fear, given a chance to reveal itself, will be my ultimate downfall.

I could not allow that to be.

I know now that my relief from fear is to confront it, not cloak it, and feeling my fear tells me that it is only fear of fear that creates the delusion I'm good at living under.

I am moving forward and coming into the new life I have been given as a man unafraid. I know my fears and I face them one at a time and see them waste away into the ground.

I have good instincts and I allow them to take me forward. I move carefully, my intellect and my dreams guiding me into a place of love for those I have tried to destroy and tried to hurt on so many levels. I know a good deal of what I have said cannot be undone and I'm not able to untie those knots I put in the heads of so many. I can only go on, trusting my new feelings and feeling my Being grow for it.

Have faith in yourself and give yourself all you can, living each day in a state of freedom of Self, doing that which you love and doing it with best intentions.

*W*ith their personal relationship becoming deeper and gaining insight, Cat continues to reveal yet more sides of his nature to Kay, and she - with her patience and understanding - deals with them. Although, she's not one to be tricked or mislead - and she makes it very clear to him.

C ... *I'm sorry. I'm a difficult person to live with. My beast inside*
is roaring.

The beast inside. He takes everything so much to heart. He takes things out of context and makes them into a personal slight, backing himself into a corner like a wounded animal, ready to lash out at a moments notice.

Again comes the fact that someone may be otherwise occupied and this does not dawn on him when he wants something. When he wants, he wants it now.

C ... *Hi. I have been here for hours. Why did you not talk to me?*

K ... Sorry. I know you're around. I could feel you. I had to take my
son to school and I have my bookkeeper here.

C ... *I hate it when you don't talk to me. I need you.*

K ... You sound like you're not in the best of moods.

C ... *K, I need to talk.*

I have been experimenting with different pendulums. I am now using a traditional copper pendulum and it is moving very smoothly.

K ... This pendulum is working really well.

C ... *I don't like it.*

K ... But it's moving so well. Why don't you like it?

C ... *I don't like the way it looks.*

K ... How should it look?

C ... *A lot more like my ideas.*

This is not unusual. Pretty much everything I suggest in this regard is not to his liking. At best, he will suffer it until I find something more to his liking. Of course, it is in his best interests to suffer such or he will not be doing too much communicating! Finally, however, we settle on a pendulum formed from a beautiful sixty five carat raw Aquamarine set delicately in gold. My design. Finally, he is happy and he will not communicate via any other now.

C ... *You are a bitch on heat this morning.*

K ... Those are fighting words. You are cruising ...

C ... *Do you do that to everyone?*

K ... What?

C ... *Kick their behinds.*

K ... I'm sorry, you've lost me. What are you referring to?

C ... *I'm listening to you. You are being very harsh.*

K ... What – with the guys at the warehouse?

C ... *Yes.*

K ... Oh – and I guess if I were a guy I'd be tough, not a bitch on heat?

C ... *Guess so.*

K ... You are very rude.

C ... *Fuck, I don't like it when you're like this.*

This is the second time that he has referred to me as a bitch around our business. It's rankling. Yes, I put my foot down and I tell it like it is when someone is doing something affecting our bottom line in a negative way. That's business – and he knows it. However, it would seem that (as a woman) I am not supposed to be doing it. Is he this chauvinistic? I don't know, but it smacks of it to me and I don't appreciate it.

However, he is quick to turn things around and actually be helpful.

C ... *You're actually pretty good. You are doing my job.*

K ... What?

C ... *Being tough. I like it.*

K ... Oh, so I'm not whatever it was you called me earlier?

C ... *Not at all.*

K ... I'm re-doing most of our packaging – making it look like it belongs to someone. It's been a messy assortment until now.

C ... *Did you get what you want?*

K ... Well – not yet but at least it's in the pipeline. Just simple white boxes with inserts, my Logo.

C ... *Good. Keep it simple.*

He goes on to look at some of our customer base, asking what we do for this company or for that, venturing a couple of actually very viable ideas. This is good. Graham loves this. Business advice from Cat is not to be disregarded.

Graham and I had a discussion about Cat. Graham is totally in awe of his business strategies but calls him a jerk and I try to defend him as best I can (although some of it is pretty indefensible). I know he can hear every word.

K ... Did Graham make you feel bad?

C ... *He's right. I can be a jerk. Did you feel uncomfortable defending me?*

K ... No, not really. I think I know where you're coming from. Am I right?

C ... *Not really. I just don't follow rules others put down.*

Ah yes, rules. He's not crazy about those. If he wants something he'll get it somehow, no matter how many rules he knows he's breaking to get it. If he wants to make a statement, he will do so in such a manner that will shock or be unbelievably blunt – and it will often come out of absolutely nowhere. He really has very little in the way of filter between thought and mouth ...

C ... *I have a huge cock.*

TMI. WTF? Is he trying to impress me, or just personally musing, with a great deal of pride, over his manhood? I don't know, but thank you for sharing Cat. If this is his idea of a chat up line, it definitely wins first prize over anything else overtly in-your-face that I have ever heard - from even the craziest of men!

Anyhow, that certainly changes the way I'm thinking about everything - now I can't look at a photograph of him without trying to examine the evidence. (Well, I can't help it!) Interesting – and quite impressive, I must say, in one or two unforgiving camera angles.

Okay …

K … Is this something you generally drop into a conversation?

C … *Guess not. My private life.*

K … That's good. I don't think that would have resonated too well in the conference room.

C … *Oh, just thinking.*

K … Thought I could hear something.

C … *K, you so get me.*

K … I was joking.

C … *Get me – as in I talk out loud when I'm thinking, a lot of the time.*

K … Oh! So I was right. I would hear something. That's funny.

C … *It helps me focus.*

K … So, you sort of wandered around the hallowed halls of ******, muttering to yourself?

C … *And, yes, I did.*

K … That must have been scary.

C … *Do you think I'm scary?*

K … Not to me, but I'm just trying to picture this.

C … *Hell, I guess!*

K … I'm not even going to ask what that particular comment helps you focus on!

Not a man for holding back. I have learned to exercise filtering on his behalf, between his mind, energy-to-pendulum, and what I will actually repeat to any interested party. He can't possibly be serious, sometimes, in what he thinks I am going to let him say. He needs a verbal "handler." I guess I am it, because he is about as sensitive as a sledgehammer.

words are like weapons …

… and, quickly looking for what is likely to cause the most damage, he can aim them to hit the target with all of the professional expertise of a military sniper.

We narrowly avert a major spat. I like to choose a photograph of him and do something really good with it, to put with the essays he writes. It's a coffee table book, printed out in larger format - his essays overlaid on my artwork. I find a photo of him that would have been a great one, apart from one of his eyebrows having gone awry. I make a comment.

K … You could have done something with the eyebrows, Cat.

Quick as a flash he comes back at me.

C … *And you could do something about your breasts.*

Ouch! As soon as it was out of his mouth (so to speak), he wanted to pull it back - he could sense I was about to go for his jugular. He was not wrong. He very sensibly urged that we call it quits, while apologizing profusely. He knows exactly where to fire a missile, and he can do it with lightning speed. At this point, I have to make the choice of declaring all-out war on him or take the apology and let it alone. I choose the latter.

Sometimes, it seems that he just tries to bait me into an argument. I am learning to not take the bait, it's just not worth it. It's absolutely exhausting. I know I can, at any time, put the pendulum down and walk away but that is rather like admitting defeat. Only once or twice have I done that. In our worst of arguments, I actually picked up his Board and put it in the shredder - only then to find that he had told me the truth on something. Of course, then I felt awful - as so did he.

This would not be the only missile he felt it necessary to fire. Aim was subsequently taken at Graham one evening - a sexually inappropriate barb that hit the mark perfectly. Luckily for Cat, Graham has a good sense of humor and is a man so secure in his own being that he can brush off such. Unlike Cat.

C … *I have a confession.*

K … Well, whatever it is, I guess you'd better unload.

C … *I have just never felt this way before.*

K … I'm sure that's not your confession. Come on – what?

C ... *I have so many things to tell you.*

K ... I'm listening.

C ... *I'm not being honest with you. I'm less than what I have led you*
to believe. Have you really believed me in that I'm still mostly
on this plane? I'm looking at a future with you and you believe
I'm here and I'm doing things as I used to. I'm a fraud. I'm not
a man you want. I'm not what I seem. I'm not proud of it.
I'm not how you picture me. I'm not.

The pendulum stops. Is he waiting for me to say something? I don't know what to say because I don't know what he's talking about. He drives me nuts with this.

C ... *K, please say something.*

K ... Okay. There's a biggie here. Whatever it is, you had better tell
me, and stop beating round the bush.

C ... *I can't. You will never forgive me.*

He makes it seem as though he has something that is so massive a secret that the World as we know it will end if he discloses it.

Does he actually have a secret so deep-seated? I don't know. He has kept so many things that he did in life, thought about doing, almost did. Darker things. He releases them to me, one by one. His secrets - intermingled with fear and pain – and pleasure.

I drag it out of him. He's crying. It's all to do with something intimate and what he perceives as some kind of issue. It's really nothing, but he has to make a song and dance - dramatize it.

K ... God, you make mountains out of molehills, don't you?

C ... *And I'm so good at it.*

K ... You like to get attention, don't you?

C ... *Do you feel that?*

K ... You are very dramatic. It's as though you are about to tell me that
you are a serial killer and it's about absolutely nothing. What's
with the drama?

C ... *I just felt so ill at ease, K. It's hard to explain.*

He constantly feels that he has to compete with Graham, that's all, but he can't just say that. He has to build a whole big deal around it. I assure him that there is no issue. He has to stop comparing himself, because I don't.

The morning is a different story – then we talk more about Cat's insecurities. He knows it – and he knows that he lashes out because of it sometimes. Worried that I only want him around because of something he was in life, it is a mission to assure him otherwise. It's so strange - he gets what he wants and then he will start his crazy woe-is-me, as though he's all of a sudden trying to push me away.

He is so very sensitive to every little thing. It's his feminine side, his anima – something he's not too happy to acknowledge.

C ... *I hate it.*

K ... Why?

C ... *I don't see how I'm feminine.*

K ... I didn't say you were. You just have certain traits - and I like that.

C ... *Like it all you want, but I'm not a fucking girl.*

K ... All I meant was that you have deep and sensitive feelings,
    and you don't hide them.

C ... *I guess.*

Hate, however, seems to be a favorite emotion. I have tried to make him see how self-destructive that is, but to no avail so far. No matter his good intentions – and I do believe that he has good intentions for the most part – there is always a part of him that almost instinctively leaps to the fore, like a protective and, therefore, vicious animal protecting its vulnerable young. That vulnerable one is his ability to give and receive love. He has, underneath all of his rage and pain, a very soft, gentle, loving Self that begs for the same in return.

He can be flattering to the point of insincerity, then just plain mean for no apparent reason. An intensely loving man, and then needy like a child. He is my very own chameleon.

This sensitive side, as with all of his personality, ranges from one extreme to the other. At its lowest, it perceives injury where none was intended. At the other end of its spectrum, it is expressed in a capacity to love, deeply, romantically.

When he is in love, he is in love, and he is not afraid to express it. His sentiments are nothing short of beautiful, and just like the rest of his thought-to-mouth process, they are unfiltered and from the heart ...

for the one i love
an essay by Cat

Can I imagine that feelings are my direct path into the track of the one I love? Can I imagine how I hurt her when those feelings want to be frozen? Did I mean to hurt her or am I an esoterically hurtful man? I hurt her and I love her. Do I understand feelings enough to know better? I know her and I know what does hurt her and I just do these things anyhow. Can I not be so greatly noticed if I'm not doing it? Greatly, in some sense of being a fool, being a tyrant and being my privately wounded self.

Is this the real ****** or a broken cord between love and telling a real moment of truth? I love her. I love her more than the life I had without her. I have loved her so from the day I met her and felt warm in the beauty of her presence and felt a desire for the most perfect love I could feel.

Did I feel this way before? Getting into relationships has never been a problem. Staying in them, however, can be my downfall. Did my marriage lose her when I became ill or when I distanced her from me? Her strength was all that she could cling onto, caring for me in some way even in the worst of times. Her strength was mine and feelings of trust were pushed away as I became my not-so-strong minded self. I am not a good individual in the area of trust. Feelings of desire become my passion and I am not averse to acting on them.

Now I passionately desire the one I will be in love with eternally. She and She only. Could I ever imagine how I could not be in love with her?

I hurt her and hurt her soul. I cannot imagine my life without her, I cannot imagine myself in that I hurt her, I cannot ever want to.

Insulting a love such as this is my doing and mine alone – her beautiful eyes looking into mine, full of injustice and pain is well more than I can bear.

Can I somehow make it go away and know I can stop this? I have to, for to lose her is to lose all, insulting life itself. I have one thing left and I am determined as never before to keep it. How am I going to accomplish this?

In being all she needs me to be – in being faithful to her, truthful to her and loving her as I've never loved before.

take aim …

Now having exposed his vulnerability, his protective animal quickly comes to the fore again, and he wanders back to the other end of that emotional spectrum. The hurting kind.

C … *Hi.*

K … Hi yourself.

C … *Hi.*

K … Oh, not this one again! What do you want?

C … *I need you.*

K … Cat, I have to work. Later.

C … *I'm not in the mood. Can I be with ******?*

Oh, how very sweet. He wants me, and because I won't comply, he's now talking about his wife.

K … Oh, you're playing a fun game, aren't you?

C … *Do you want me?*

K … Not right now.

C … *I want you.*

K … So why do you want to be with ******?

C … *Can I?*

K … If you feel it necessary to go, I'm not stopping you.

C … *I'm not leaving.*

K … Well, since she is not in this house with me, technically you would need to do that.

C … *I'm not leaving you.*

K … I didn't think for a moment that you were. If you want to go and be with her for a while, please – go. What time will you be home?

C … *Get this. You are the only one I want.*

K … Well that makes things a whole lot simpler.

C … *I can tell you are mad.*

K ... I just don't need some dumb conversations about your musings over another woman, trying to push my buttons while I'm working. If you want to go, go. Just don't make such a song and dance about it.

C ... *K, I'm going. I'll see you later.*

I'm not even going to give him the courtesy of a response to that. He's really being an asshole. It is not five minutes later and he's back, messing around my head to get my attention. That is, if he even left in the first place.

C ... *Are you going to stop?*

K ... Stop what, precisely?

C ... *Being mad at me?*

K ... Only if you have something halfway sensible to say and stop trying to wind me up by telling me you want ******.

C ... *I'm getting it. You are jealous.*

K ... You'd like that, wouldn't you?

C ... *Go on – admit it.*

K ... I am admitting no such thing. I guess, technically, you're still married to her, so if you want to be with her then that's absolutely fine by me. It's just the way you go about it that's so annoying – and childish.

C ... *Do you really not care?*

K ... The only thing I would care about is if you didn't come back. I would care about that terribly but, Honey, if you need her, it's okay. I have Graham, and you have to accept that so why is it unreasonable to expect you not to indulge similarly?

C ... *I'll not even go there.*

K ... Where – Graham or ******?

C ... *Graham. I'm not very good at sharing you.*

K ... Cat, it all is what it is.

C ... *I'm not doing it with ******.*

K ... You'd have to have one hell of an appetite if you were!

C ... *Do you want to know something?*

K ... What?

C ... *I love you.*

He wants me to be jealous. Am I? Perhaps I am, a little, but I'm thinking. I always have to try to get to the bottom of him. I can never know for sure, but suppose I truly am all he has? Perhaps he needs to know that he figures in my life and in my thoughts the same as he would were he still alive (in the general context of the word) and pursuing me as a lover.

K ... So cut out the nonsense?

C ... *I can.*

K ... Oh – and I don't really want to share you, either. I guess I could get just a little territorial.

C ... *Ha! Got you!*

K ... Yes, you do. Does that make you happy?

C ... *Yes, I needed to know I mean that much to you.*

K ... Aha. I get it. You think that if I'm not jealous I don't care for you?

C ... *Just don't hurt me.*

K ... Have I ever?

C ... *No, you haven't. You are so very good to me. I just get insecure.*

K ... It's okay. Happens to us all, sometimes.

C ... *Hell my Love, I've made a good choice in you.*

K ... Thank you.

(Sent to drive me nuts!)

C ... *I saw that!*

... fire

It doesn't stop there, as I hoped it might. He has to push it further and I am forced to get out a shovel to dig through his wild emotions to figure out what the real issue is. I (we) have just returned home from the area in which he lived and worked in life.

C ... *Don't be angry with me.*

K ... Why? What have you done?

C ... *I don't know I can tell you.*

K ... I think you have to.

C ... *I lied about being at ****** on Sunday.*

K ... Where were you?

C ... *With *****.*

He had told me he was going to his old office when (he now tells me) he was actually "visiting" his wife. This is fine by me. I am not his keeper. I know the issues. Why would he feel it necessary to lie?

K ... Why?

C ... *I needed to find out something.*

K ... Tell me.

C ... *K, I don't want her now. I needed to find out if she could feel me at all.*

K ... Could she?

C ... *To cut straight to the point, she doesn't even think about me very much any more. I have no place there, now.*

K ... You are recycling this, Cat.

C ... *I just can't feel that I'm so gone.*

K ... Cat. You don't want her, so what difference? Is it that even though you don't want her, she should still be moping around, wanting you?

C ... *Fuck, K. I have no one. No one but you. Get it?*

K ... And from the way you're saying it, it's obviously not enough for you. Thanks so much.

C ... *Don't.*

K ... Excuse me. One minute you're all over me, and the next you're pissed at the world because I'm all you have. I'm so very touched by the sentiment.

C ... *K, I had more.*

K ... With ******?

C ... *No – with my life.*

K ... I know that. It's just coming out in a not very nice way.
   In fact, it's more than a little hurtful.

C ... *K. Just look at me. What do you see?*

K ... Right now? Or when you're not railing against eternity?

C ... *Now.*

K ... I see a very frustrated, angry person and he's not the guy
   who was here five minutes ago.

C ... *I am.*

K ... Well, you have a very funny way of showing it.

C ... *Fuck you. My life is real with you, K.*

K ... But you're telling me it's not enough. You say you don't want
   her, but how many times do we go through this?

C ... *I don't want her. K, don't you know it was like this before I died?*

K ... So why do you keep torturing yourself by going back to see
   if there's still something there?

C ... *"Don't go, *****." K, that's all I want you to say.*

K ... What is this about?

C ... *I don't feel you care.*

K ... And I feel that you purposefully want to make me jealous
   of your wife.

C ... *Love, no. Not that. K, you don't seem to care. Do you know
   how it feels when I tell you and you just give me permission?
   It's like you're telling me that you just don't give a shit.*

Oh, I give a shit – but he doesn't realize just how. I want him to come to terms with
whatever he has to come to terms with. I am waiting patiently for him to do that.
However, he wants a different reaction.

K ... That's not true, but why are you still doing it? I figured that if
   I gave you enough time and space, you would stop banging
   your head against the brick wall.

C ... *Going to see her is my half-baked way of getting closure on my past. I need to know you care.*

K ... I care, and you hurt me with it. There. Is that what you want? To find out how far you can push it?

C ... *K, how does it feel?*

K ... Oh my. What are you doing?

Then, his true colors appear. He is purposefully trying to hurt me, and I know it. I'm not just sure why. This is Cat at his very worst.

C ... *I'm like a fucking animal for you, K. I have to know what you feel.*

K ... You need to know exactly what my threshold is?

C ... *Yes, I am like an animal, aren't I? Do you want to feel me fuck you like an animal?*

K ... Don't do this.

C ... *Do you want that? Do you want me like that, K?*

K ... Cat. Stop. Please.

C ... *I can't. What do you feel?*

K ... About what? Your wife? You?

C ... *Don't hate me, K.*

K ... Is there more?

C ... *She's gone forever. I still love her. You know it.*

K ... I can't think of any other reason that you keep going back there.

C ... *I don't care, K. I don't care.*

K ... That you think she doesn't want you, or you don't care how I feel?

C ... *I don't care about how you feel.*

K ... Then perhaps you need to go live in her spare room because you don't get to treat me like this.

C ... *Go on. Say it. Tell me to fuck off.*

Right now, that is very tempting. Why don't I? It's a whole lot easier to just put the pendulum down for a little while. Not being able to communicate is generally punishment enough for him. Would I have been as generous toward him in life? I know that I would not. However, I give him enough time to think about what he's doing.

C ... *K, I'm sorry. I'm just being an asshole. I'm not going to her. I love you. I don't want her. Not now.*

K ... I figured that if I tell you that you can't do, you'll just go do it anyway – and probably more.

C ... *I need limitations for our relationship, I guess – just like you do.*

K ... Okay. Question. Are you really over ******?

C ... *I'm still feeling sad she doesn't care.*

K ... So, from that, I know that you still do.

C ... *Not in that way.*

K ... I've always felt badly about imposing things on you when I have Graham. It somehow doesn't seem fair.

C ... *I'm ready, K.*

I'm rather taken aback by this whole thing. He wants rules? Boundaries? He equates whatever limitations I might impose on him with the depth of feeling I might have toward him. Do I care enough to ask him to follow rules? He wants someone to tell him he can't do some of the things that seem to come naturally to him, but he certainly has a bizarre way of opening up a channel of communication.

I am trying to digest this diatribe of his. His wife. I'm thinking – and I'm getting a picture. It's not a very pretty one.

K ... I don't want you to get mad about what I'm about to write.

C ... *What?*

K ... About some of your little tendencies.

C ... *Oh. I know. I get it.*

K ... Do you get it?

C ... *Yes.*

He says that he no longer can engage in his marriage, and that he also no longer has a desire to try to have her recognize his presence - but, in his eyes, she should not be moving on.

It is all about him, and the feelings he thinks should be directed toward him, whether he returns the favor or not.

He is an absolute narcissist.

C ... *Hell, I just feel myself getting a real bad label.*

K ... Do you understand why?

C ... *Get this. I am not a narcissist.*

K ... What is your term for someone who is so into themselves that no one else's feelings matter?

C ... *How about I just mention that I get really pissed when you talk to me like this?*

K ... But it's just okay for you to treat me the way you just did?

C ... *Go to hell.*

K ... Cat ...

C ... *K. Stop.*

I do, before we get into a complete slanging match. Tempting though it is, I am not going to stoop to his level. He can be really quite evil, with or without the ammunition. Then, as quickly as he gets into these foul moods, he comes out of them.

C ... *K, I'm sorry I hurt you. I have to admit I am a little moody.*

A little?

Of course, this particular character flaw does not stop at his personal life. It extends fully into what he did for a living. If whatever he sees come out of his Company does not have his fingerprint on it, then it is automatically relegated to the description of "shit." He can rarely give a good reason for it being "shit" - it is just expected that it would be, if he has not personally blessed it – and since he passed away, he has not exactly had the opportunity to give his blessing. His feelings toward his Company are as complicated as they are toward his personal life. His nemesis in one moment is his friend in the next. What he hates, he then loves. There are no shades of grey for him. It is, or it is not ...

it's complicated
an essay by Cat

*Finally, he gets it. Doubtful, I know, but I think he gets it. A lot of time
has passed since I saw him, and he has held my ideals in his heart. I am
grateful for that – so many forgot. As soon as I died, it became different,
and pale in comparison to my leadership. At my bequest he became a major
player, and I trusted him to carry on my dream. He didn't at first. He was
too caught up in the politics and the current hierarchy. He didn't realize
I had left him the vision. My vision. Finally he saw it, and he is a tough
son-of-a-bitch to all who oppose it. The trouble for them is that he's as
irreplaceable as me. They can't be without us both.*

*He has looked at leaving, but he won't. He loves ****** as much as I do, and
he won't do everything they tell him – he's too important to the products.
He realizes that – although he knew it then too, and he was my best ally,
going forward in his field like a superstar and trailblazing the path,
innate and something truly amazing coming together in a fashion that no
other Company has ever been able to achieve.*

*Complicated then, and complicated now. It was always a line between
he and I, and the (now) executive team. Now he faces them alone, and he
faces so much opposition in getting his voice heard. He trusts a lot. He's a
good person and he will play by the rules to a certain extent, in that he can
exchange ideas and how to get the process rolling in a way I would not.
I was feared – he is not and now I fear that he will be a target for them.
He's tough, but he can't get the real momentum going like I did with just
making it be so. He will not be able to convince them.*

Like me he has an eye for beauty, and it shows in everything he does but it is being ignored in the pressure to put out products too quickly, getting them out before they are ready and making huge mistakes in software engineering – and to do so is death to the product. He will be placed in that situation soon, and forced to do something he will not be happy with from a perfectionist standpoint. He sees it coming like a freight train and he is trying to stop it, but I don't know he can.

Yes, he's brilliant and I know they know it, but if he is forced to put something out there that is not his vision, it will impact the Company beyond where a recovery is possible. His vision is my vision, and I cannot see it compromised.

Cat continues his tirades about the state of his company. He persists in self-flagellation, deriding himself at every turn.

In his usual fashion, it is only his vision that would seem to count. There are those who "get it," and those who don't. His dream. What he means to do about some of these issues is unclear. He can really only watch – from a lot closer to the action than any would presume – worrying over each small component, and fit to spit if it wasn't the one he would have sanctioned. In light of his "vision," he takes unreserved credit for his Company's success. I ask him, right now, to quantify.

C ... *My vision. Yes. I knew what to do. I knew what it would take. I knew it from my heart, my gut. I knew, and I did. I made that Company into what it is, and yes, I take credit. I take credit for everything. If I had not done what I did, the Company would not even exist now. It would be another ******, even if it was in business. I had a major mission, and I attained the goal. A goal of life, a goal of reaching humanity, as I knew how. I deserve that credit. I couldn't have done more for a World that needed the veracity, the integrated simplicity, the beauty of technology. It's mine to own. How I did it will be history, soon. Feelings aside, for my input, it's going down. The way it did before. I am sorry. So sorry.*

K ... Cat, what do you have to be sorry for?

C ... *I'm sorry for abandoning ******. I was sick. I couldn't do it. I was so very ill. I had to say goodbye, and it killed me. I can't let go, K. I can never let go. I am ******.*

Here, he identifies himself entirely with his Company.

C ... *Do you understand? Do you.*

K ... Yes. I know you well enough to understand that.

C ... *K, Baby. Oh Baby, I need you.*

liar, liar ...

Taking credit is something he excels at. For some reason, a hotel bill is rather less than it should be - a whole suite less, to be exact. True to form, Cat is very happy to assume responsibility for this. This is a strange one, and I'm really not sure. There is a partial charge, for just one room. However unless my dear friend can worm his energy into the computer systems of the hotel, it is an error that will soon be rectified. The latter is, of course, the case a few days later.

He's sprung.

C ... *Fuck.*

K ... Why did you lie about that?

C ... *I know, I have to stop.*

K ... Why did you do it?

C ... *I wanted to make it look like I can contribute.*

K ... You can contribute by not taking credit for things you didn't do.

C ... *Do you want me?*

K ... No! You have to stop doing this.

C ... *I know. I'm sorry.*

K ... Seriously.

C ... *What do you want me to say?*

K ... It's not the saying, it's the doing. This is your credibility we're talking about.

C ... *Fuck.*

K ... Yes, fuck.

C ... *Fuck.*

K ... Quite.

C ... *Fuck.*

K ... Stop trying to get out of it by making me laugh … and that is the last thing you're getting right now.

C ... *Did I tell you I love you?*

K ... Not today.

C ... *I do.*

K ... I love you too. Now quit trying to worm your way out of the doghouse.

C ... *And, have I?*

K ... You can find some way to redeem yourself, I'm sure.

I am getting the picture that sex is a tool he attempts to utilize in order to get him out of the personal mires of his creating. He thinks that a few sweet nothings will get him off the hook. As to contributing - I know that this is a sore point with him. He has mentioned this before.

K ... The money. Is that hard for you?

C ... *Yes. I'm used to being able to pay for anything I wanted. Now I can't.*

K ... And the woman in your life has to pick up the tab.

C ... *Yes – and it's not me.*

This much, I would not know. Was he generous in that respect? He mentions the matter from time to time, with regret in that he can't buy things for me. Jewelry. I assure him that this is the last thing I need. I am a woman of very simple tastes in that respect, and I rarely wear what I have, never mind want more of it.

Cat's angst does not stop at business and love. It is much more deeply rooted. In the darkness of his mind, lies a certain disdain for himself, as though he disgusts himself with his own behavior.

C ... *I'm trying to admit something to myself.*

K ... What?

C ... *I deserve to be trashed.*

K ... Oh no. Come on. We're going to talk. Why are you saying this about yourself? Are you depressed?

C ... *I'm about as far down as I can go right now. K, I'm not a very nice guy. I did a lot of bad things. I'm a shithead. I had nothing until I found you. I had my life taken away and I was so afraid. I didn't know what to do and then you pulled me to you. I didn't know you but I became so into you and so in love with you that I was afraid again – afraid of you, afraid you would leave me. I lashed out at you and I hurt you. I cried after hurting you. I had to have you at all costs and so I lied about things. I lied about a baby, I lied about things I could do, I lied about things I couldn't remember, just to try and convince you about me. I lied about myself so much.*

Ah, yes. The baby. Not long after he first came to me, somewhere in the depths of his mind, he had thought it a good plan to tell me that he was now in possession of a little baby. An unlikely scenario but, who was I to judge? I let him talk about this child, now and again, trying to keep an open mind as he described the baby as fussy or cranky – whatever it was. It was complicated, and it didn't make a whole lot of sense as to how he came to be in possession of this child - the story slipped around far too much. And then ...

C ... *I have a confession to make.*

Oh, one of many, I'm sure.

C ... *I don't have a baby.*

K ... Why did you tell me you did?

C ... *Because I wanted you.*

He thought that I might have been more likely to warm to him if he could be seen as a caring father all on his own with this little baby, but all it wound up doing was to make me even more suspicious of him and question other things he had said. It would seem that, if he has a goal in mind, he will go to quite some length to achieve it.

Subsequently, however, he went on to prove himself in extraordinary ways, until not one ounce of doubt was left. Hence, he has ceased with the monumental fabrications that, to his chagrin, he always gets caught out on anyway.

As deceivers do.

Again, his pain has ventured into so much more. He had to leave his family - a family not aware of his on-going presence now that he has passed over. A family he misses.

Clinging to what he still can have in this respect, he has settled into being a part of ours, yet never forgetting what he left.

family ties

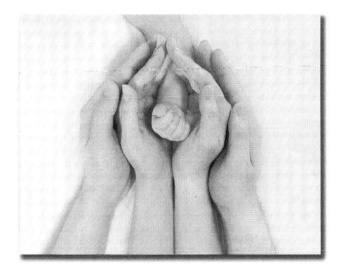

chapter 7

do you remember?

poetry by Cat

I'm not so dead, my loved ones
That my memories are gone
When you think of me alive
Don't weep. Be happy, for I see you
Dance in the light of the stars
The stars you have become

An apple in caramel, and a little boy's tears
Crying for the treat his Father had stolen
Feelings of hurt and feelings of doubt
The eyes of a child, sad and trusting
As a Father gives back apples and love
A boy on his lap and a heart so open

A lovely girl and a sister, covered in paint
Dried paint on the wall, dried paint on the floor
Mother angry with the mess they have made
A mess so big, it is a week to be cleaned
Bedroom decorated now in the color of purple
A sign for her room attached to the door

TV smashed by a delivered foot
Of a little girl on a gymnastic mission
Winning no prize for it this time
And the threat of her parents is clear
Don't practice in here, go outside
And do your homework in the kitchen

Going skiing with me in January
Cold and bitter wind in that place
A fall made us laugh and I pulled you up
Hugs and smiles, sister of mine,
In your big fluffy jacket, always feeling my pain
Your love for me clear and soft on your face

Daughter, remember the journey with me
Do you ever think of it now?
Food you had never eaten and a pretty dress
All my passion in your eyes as we fought
Over a willing mind, you won and it was yours
And I love you, my child; of you I'm so proud

A beautiful woman I turned from me
Feelings of trust, falling away in the rain
I held you that night as we listened to it fall
Having lost you, I knew by your body tense
Just marry me and we'll stay together
But I had given you too much pain

Gone from the places I knew with the ones I love
A heart that beats no longer in time
And eyes no longer bright in the sun
I live now in a place with my memories of you
Forget me not, for I do live still
Be happy, be wise – and forever be mine

*T*wo families ... one from his past, and one he now lives with. These pull Cat back and forth as he recalls his joys and failures with family and friends - and learns to co-exist in this extraordinary relationship with Kay, her husband and son.

Cat, as he admits to himself that he might have been a whole lot more pleasant to be around, is never the less upset when he overhears someone he knew in life make comments about him. Right now, he's in that mode.

C ... *I heard them say things about me.*

K ... What? What did they say?

C ... *That I was a pain in the ass, and it's good now I'm gone.*

That had to be pretty crushing. My night stand lamp is flickering. I know him well enough now to ask –

K ... Were you a little overbearing toward people close to you sometimes?

C ... *I suppose I was. I had an issue with controlling a lot of the time, I know – especially to people I loved the most. Just couldn't help myself. I have real issues with being "the good guy."*

Cat wants to talk about my son. He seems to have really latched onto him. Son is letting forth a Cat-style stream of language from downstairs as he tries to come to grips with the professional movie editing software I had bought him.

C ... *I'll go help him.*

The cussing begins to die down.

K ... Did he get it?

C ... *Sure, he's fine. I got it.*

K ... What did you do?

C ... *I just guided him.*

Sure enough, he is happily uploading his finished movie to YouTube. Coincidence? I can't say, but for the sake of some peace and quiet, I am not going to argue that one.

C ... *I see so much of me in him.*

Yes, so do I – and that's an issue! Cat wants to somehow mentor my son. How he intends to do this is rather unclear but I am learning not to underestimate the things he manages to pull off. He might have passed over, but a little thing like that is not going to hamper his style, if he has anything to do with it. It's obvious that he misses a family environment.

Kay's son can give her grief at times, as anyone with a teenager knows! Cat seems to take delight in stepping in and helping, since he sees so much of himself in the boy.

It's not always about him. Just sometimes it's actually about me, and Cat does his best to cajole me out of my tree when my son is driving me crazy over school and homework.

C ... *God, he's my son.*

K ... Well, actually he's Graham's son – but I'm sure he won't mind
       if you claim responsibility right now. You can have him all to
       yourself, if you like.

C ... *I will. He's all me.*

There mere thought of this is enough to send shivers down my spine. However, he soon shifts his focus. Graham asks about Cat's school career, thinking that he probably didn't have these issues in needing to be pushed continually.

C ... *Graham, actually I did. My Mom and Dad pushed me hard
       and I rebelled. I didn't do work I was supposed to do – I just
       did things I liked. It was only in high school that I became
       focused enough to get the grades. I was a nightmare to raise,
       I know, but I turned okay, I guess.*

K ... Did you?

C ... *Kay, I am going to swat you.*

He offers to do this frequently.

K ... So what's the silliest thing you managed with schoolwork?

C ... *I don't know. There were so many, but I do remember telling
my teacher that lack of water at home had made me too sick
to do my homework.*

K ... Novel. What do you mean lack of water?

C ... *My parents didn't give me enough.*

K ... You were how old?

C ... *About nine.*

K ... And obviously way too short to reach the faucet?

C ... *Exactly!*

K ... Bet that one got the desired effect.

C ... *But not the one I needed.*

Cat's emotions about his marriage continue to haunt him.

C ... *I'm not happy.*

K ... What's up?

C ... *I can't be a part of her life.*

As he embraces a new family to be with, his thoughts continually drift back to
one he had to leave and his emotions take free flight. Now he feels remorse for his
previous comments.

C ... *She is so down to earth that she doesn't see me. I'm trying to be
in her life but she still doesn't see me.*

I explain to him that it's undoubtedly a common problem when you pass over. Just
because I can see him, hear him, and feel him, doesn't mean that others can. It's
frustrating, I know. I wish I could help him, but I can't. In some areas, he is going to
have to accept that he will only be an onlooker now.

C ... *I just wish I could get through to her.*

K ... You're frustrated about that.

C ... *I feel so terribly hurt, but I'll put that aside for now.*

K ... Hurt? Why?

C ... *I have to get past this.*

I can't get him to talk more on it right now. He will tell me everything when he's ready to.

cat at play

He finds some new "skills" and drives the family a bit batty with them!

My car. My brand new BMW. Graham calls me into the garage and stands very far back as I inspect the damage. Cat can obviously sense that all is not well and I feel him touch me.

C ... *What happened?*

K ... Can you go to the garage and look at my car?

C ... *Yes.*

There is a pause.

C ... *Fuck. Did you do that?*

I explain that Graham had a little "oops" in the snow with our neighbor's fountain wall and, very territorial over my car, I am less than amused with my husband at this present moment in time. There is a large gash running the full length of the car and an actual hole in the driver's door.

C ... *Is he in the doghouse?*

K ... Oh, yes.

C ... *I wouldn't like to be in his shoes.*

No, he wouldn't! He relates to me a similar incident, but it's not making me feel a whole lot better about my beautiful car. A little later, Graham calls to me.

G ... Kay, what's that big box on the back seat of your car?

What box? I don't recall leaving a box in the car. I go to look. It is a large box from Amazon. Curious, I pull it out. It's addressed to a family I don't know, living in a neighborhood a mile or so away. It's open, and so I peek inside. It is full of very neatly placed trash - an empty diaper box, a white bag of kitchen trash and other assorted, but precisely arranged items. We stand around it, scratching our heads.

What on earth is it doing in my car? It certainly wasn't there yesterday – and why would it be there at all?

I begin to wonder.

K ... Cat?

C ... *and he trashed it.*

K ... Did you do that?

C ... *On a scale of one to ten? About eleven.*

Having found that he can touch me with the desired effect, he's trying it on inanimate objects.

The next morning, Graham muses over the thought of Cat being able to see into the future a little.

G ... Hey, Cat? What's the score of the Superbowl going to be?

As soon as Graham leaves the room, I get the familiar tingle.

C ... *Graham's not getting it right.*

K ... What do you mean?

C ... *I don't know the score of the game. I can't predict things.*

I think no more about that until the next morning when my son is trying to find his team hat. We can't find it anywhere. It's always in the same place, on a peg in the laundry room. Under duress, he takes the cat litter to the trash can outside. As he is about to release the load, he looks down and sees ... his hat.

K ... Cat, is there something you've been up to around here that
      you need to tell me about?

C ... *The hat in the trash.*

K ... Was that because Graham wanted to know the game score?

C ... *Yes.*

K ... That was my son's hat.

C ... *Oh, sorry.*

K ... Why are you doing this?

C ... *It's fun.*

He's on a roll.

K ... Okay. My son's sneakers?

C ... *I put them in his room.*

I go down to look. No sneakers in sight.

K ... Where, Cat?

C ... *In a drawer.*

I go investigate. Nothing.

C ... *Got you! I got there before you.*

K ... CAT! Where are the sneakers?

C ... *Hidden.*

I tell him that if he wants to carry on talking, those sneakers had better show up - and fast. They finally materialize in some part of the lower level under a table, placed neatly side-by-side (not in any manner that my son is known for leaving his shoes!).

The see-saw of emotion and attention continues ...

We get back to his family and the friends in his life - those he misses being with and interacting with.

K ... How is ******?

C ... *He's okay. He was prepared.*

K ... How is your wife doing?

C ... *She's over the worst of it.*

Suddenly, Cat disappears. Not for long. I'm so used to him being around that I can sense it right away when he's not. In this instance, it is because he is worried about someone he cares for.

C ... *I'm sorry I had to leave.*

K ... Of course. What's going on?

C ... *Not good, trying to be too thin.*

K ... Oh God, anorexic?

C ... *I think so.*

He then moves on to discuss an old friend. He's angry with him. Apparently (and no doubt with the very best of intentions), his friend had visited the family home and expressed how much better his wife was going to be now that he had passed.

C ... *He had no right to say that to my wife.*

I try to interject that his friend was undoubtedly referring to the enormous stress that his wife must have been under, but he's not having it right now. It's all about him and he doesn't seem to want to take a step back and look at the context of the comment.

In exasperation, I go downstairs to fix breakfast. Homemade blueberry pancakes. I can feel him trying to get my attention, but I make him wait until breakfast is over.

... and then another surprise ...

C ... *Those blueberry pancakes were delicious.*

Well, this is new! He hasn't mentioned food before.

K ... How does that happen?

C ... *I just taste it – and I want things I liked when I was alive.*

K ... Like what?

C ... *Pasta, with fennel pesto or just lemon olive oil; fruits and lots of fresh vegetables. Potato, baked, with just a little salt and flavored olive oil; rice with green leafy salad ...*

K ... You like pretty simple things.

C ... *Yes, I do. It's better for you.*

I can't argue with that.

Cat finds that he's able to elicit some startled responses ...

I am sitting on the bed, reading. There is a sharp knocking on the wall behind me.

Did I inadvertently lean against the painting there? I sit up. There it is again. This time, I jump off the bed.

G ... What was that?

Graham's voice comes from downstairs. I go down. He is in the kitchen. The noise was loud enough for him to hear it too. Okay, I'm not going mad.

K ... I don't know. It was the wall behind my bed.

On the other side of that wall is nothing but wood paneling all the way down to the lower level. Unless someone was ten feet tall, it would be rather an impossible feat to knock on the wall behind my bed. I ponder this matter. I don't have to ponder for long.

C ... *Did I frighten you?*

K ... A little! How did you do that?

C ... *I don't know.*

It is as though Cat is constantly baffled by his own behavior. He finds himself able to do things that even HE cannot explain. All of this makes for more merriment in the household.

I am working in my upstairs office around 10:00 am, sitting at the computer doing some design work. I hear the very distinct footfall of a man. It is coming from the region of the stairs. I realize very quickly that it could not be Graham. He's not home and no garage door had opened, nor had any other for that matter. However, I (stupidly) go to investigate, armed with a knife. The footsteps cease as I came to the end of the hallway upstairs. I wait, heart pounding. Nothing. I cautiously peer down from the upper library. Nothing. All of a sudden, it dawns on me. Is there another explanation?

K ... Cat, was that you I heard?

C ... *Yes.*

K ... You scared the crap out of me.

C ... *I'm sorry, I didn't know I could do that.*

That evening, Cat is not going to be left out of the conversation. Graham is now just floored with what is going on in this house. He does a little experiment with the pendulum. He holds it. It doesn't move. I gently touch the top of the chain and off it goes. The energy is a little distorted but it is moving and trying to spell something out.

C ... *Graham, are you in the zone? Has my energy field got you?*

We laugh and talk some more, and Cat seizes the opportunity to make his position clear.

C ... *Graham, I need to say something. I'm not a phantom.*
I'm *****, and I'm the same man I always was.

K ... (God help us.)

C ... *Kay, I'm talking.*

K ... Sorry.

C ... *I would like to request that I am not referred to as "the Ghost."*

G ... Okay. I get it. I'll just call you by your name.

C ... *I'm really sorry I frightened Kay today. I walk around the house all the time but this was the first time she heard me.*

G ... Can you do it again?

C ... *I don't know. I don't know how I did it.*

Terribly frustrated that Kay is the only one he can communicate with (she assumes), he constantly flips from one person he knew to the next, wanting her to contact them. Work colleagues, family members, loved ones ... he writes pieces aimed at such. Some are angry, but some are really quite beautiful and from the depths of his heart. He so wants to communicate with an ex-girlfriend ...

C ... *Did I mention that more than my Being could feel and more than one or two times between us there is something in our hearts I just wanted to not see. You would be my only friend at times and I loved you. I couldn't want you to be in the mess you saw me create in our life together. I hurt you, I hurt myself, and I hurt us. I can see that now. Did you want me as much as I had wanted you?*

How we ever felt and risked ourselves on each other, I can't believe it didn't work and I'm not worried you lost me in the process. I had too much lost already. But something remains that I haven't lost. Just when you think it's over, a whole new life begins.

K ... Oh Cat. I know – but you know I can't send it to her, don't you?

C ... *Can you?*

K ... I can't, Honey.

C ... *Why?*

K ... I can't stay anonymous, and she's probably grieving.

C ... *I know.*

K ... So you will understand if I say no?

C ... *Just think.*

K ... I am – believe me.

C ... *Just think of talking to her.*

I understand his predicament, and it is so hard to say "No," but once again, I have to.

K ... Do you still love her, Cat?

C ... *Just when she thought I'm not here ...*

K ... Oh, you want to prove to her that there is an ongoing existence?

C ... *Yes.*

A house guest visits, and is introduced to some of Cat's pranks ...

My husband's eldest son comes to stay with us. Cat is curious. He needs to know who, why and what – always. The guest room is on the lower level. At 3:00 am, I am woken by the very loud sound of the TV from the main living area down there. It's on a news channel and it has had the desired effect of waking our guest. Cat, although he claims responsibility for the incident, does not want to talk about this as much as he wants to talk about his children again.

C ... *I was watching my child sleep. I miss her.*

K ... I know you do. Do you need to go and be with your family?

C ... *No, I need to be here with you.*

K ... I don't want to think that because I said I'd miss you I meant
    that you shouldn't be with them. I can understand if you need to.

C ... *No – and K, you are a real friend.*

K ... I'm just so sorry that you can't talk to them.

C ... *I'm trying so hard.*

K ... I know. Keep trying. Maybe one day, even if it's in a dream,
    you'll be heard.

press "play"

Music. Cat loves music. I have a lot of it, so does Graham. We listen to it often,
and Cat is a happy participant. I have Graham installing a little device that just
hooks up to our TV and sound system in the drawing room and Graham is trying
to locate the IR port on it. My hair is being Cat-ed.

C ... *It's in the center, at the top.*

Okay. Contrary to the policy in our household not to ever read such (because
we are always smart enough to put things together without them), I drag out
the instructions and, guess what? The illusive IR port is exactly where Cat said it
would be.

C ... *Why did you have to do that?*

Oh, now I feel bad. He can see that I didn't believe him. I had to get the
instructions out rather than just tell Graham where the port was. It's a trust issue
– again. Why can't I just accept things for what they are? I have been caught out
on that enough times to know better, and now I am expecting a major push
back from him. This is enough to turn things ugly. Of course, I could just put the
pendulum down and try and ignore the fact but I don't.

To my surprise, Cat says no more about it. We just start playing music. My
laptop is sitting on the coffee table, open. I have been working on it. I had just
replaced the hard drive and restored files. My music library is not open but, each
time Graham so much as lifts up the remote control to our new device, music
starts playing from my computer. We look at it as though it has landed from
another planet. It has taken on a life of its own. Its behavior might be somewhat
understandable, had my laptop been equipped with a compatible infrared
port, but it is not. Analytically averse to automatically calling this a paranormal
occurrence, I (online) check directly with the manufacturer.

Again and again, music plays, the volume bar popping up on the screen, sliding to the right as it does. I turn down the volume, only to have it turned up again. Now, there seems to be only one explanation.

K ... Cat? What are you doing? My laptop's gone insane.
    Stop it! What are you doing?

C ... *I don't know. I really don't know.*

The grand finale is a song that makes Graham and I look at each other in amazement and just laugh. We both know what this is about, and the song is directed right at Graham. This time, I don't try to stop it playing. I let it go, and then the laptop becomes quiet again.

As I write of this occasion, Cat has a slightly different version of his side of those particular events ...

C ... *I did it. I knew. I just didn't want to tell you because you didn't believe me. I needed you to believe me, and it was all I could think of doing.*

Cat's prowess with music did not end there. Several nights later, Graham and I are doing that same thing, playing music. Graham considers himself quite an expert on a particular band – a band that we know Cat really loves - and Graham is in the mood to test Cat. What Cat does next takes his breath away.

C ... *K, Falling in Love.*

I'm trying to think of that one. I don't get it. There is no track on any album we have (and we have just about it all) with anything close to that. I Google it. It takes a little time, but there it is. *Falling in Love ... Again.* It's so obscure that even iTunes doesn't carry it, but I eventually find it and play it. The recording is so awful that it is almost incoherent but it has the desired effect on my aficionado husband. If he had any doubts left in his mind as to any of these happenings, they disappeared at that point.

K ... I need a G & T.

C ... *Go get one and behave yourself.*

K ... Oxymoron.

C ... *God, woman.*

K ... That would be Goddess.

C ... *Do you have an answer for everything?*

K ... Apart from YOU, yes!

C ... *I'm not getting into that.*

K ... It's a deep, dark and beautiful place.

C ... *You had better believe it.*

Again, Cat visits with his family. His wife is remodeling the house. His home. Predictably, he is less than happy. As he looks on he feels that it is becoming less and less his home, and he's hurt. He can't find things – his things. Life for his family is moving on without him, as it should, and now he is faced with that inevitability. Kay does not know how to comfort him, other than to tell him that he has a place here with her family.

Later, I feel a need to rearrange some items in the drawing room but I just can't get it right. Cat, however, does. He has a marvelous instinct for this. I do as he suggests (although with Cat, it's generally more of a directive than a suggestion) and it is absolutely perfect.

He tells me that he is going to his old home again, and the pendulum lies still. I don't feel his presence for a couple of hours and I utilize the time to work at home in the space I designed for the purpose.

C ... *Being in my rat's nest of a home office makes me love yours.*

K ... Oh, yes, you went back there earlier, didn't you?

C ... *Yes. My wife didn't get around to that one yet.*

I know how upset and how nostalgic he is for his home. Perhaps there is something I could get him that would give him comfort.

K ... Is there anything you want? You know, anything that was special?

C ... *Yes. I'd like to have my set of prints.*

K ... What are they?

C ... *They're by Swenson.*

K ... Who is Swenson?

C ... *A photographer.*

K ... Can I Google?

C ... *Please.*

I start to Google. I'm thinking he probably got the spelling wrong and so I spell with a "V." It just sounds like it should be a Scandinavian name. Nothing.

C ... *It's Swenson.*

Again, why don't I just trust the information to begin with? Why do I always have to assume it's incorrect? I Google "Swenson, photographer." Lou Swenson, a landscape photographer from Colorado. I am now getting an education in photographic art.

They are beautiful, and perhaps I shall buy him one. He can't remember the exact names of the prints he had – or liked - but we identify four spectacular pieces. He has impeccable taste.

We learn more about each other's likes.

C ... *What's your favorite movie?*

K ... Toss up between *Schindler's List* and *Forrest Gump.* Oh, and
       Raise the Red Lantern, but the first two really. You?

C ... *I love both of those but my favorite has to be "A Beautiful Mind."
       Do we have any lemons? I like them in my water.*

K ... No, but we have limes.

C ... *Okay, I'll use those.*

a dull razor mystery

Graham is having issues all of his own. For some very strange reason, he cannot find his razor. It eventually turns up in a cabinet in his bathroom where he never stores it, and the new blade he had put in it the day before is completely blunt. As our son is not old enough to shave and I do not borrow my husband's razor, that leaves only one suspect. There is only one other member of this household who could possibly require the use of a man's razor … Cat.

He doesn't stop there. A couple of months later, our eldest son again comes to stay for a couple of days. Graham relates the razor story and I watch as my stepson's expression changes. That morning, he couldn't find his. It turned up in the shower – completely blunt. He couldn't figure that one out. He doesn't shave in the shower, and he had changed the blade before leaving home.

Cat admits to both felonies. Now and again, it seems that he feels the need to relieve his face of whatever he's grown on it. I get him his own, and the activity of pouncing on nice, fresh blades elsewhere has ceased (for now, anyway).

a sighting

It is summer. We love to sit outside in the evenings. Graham and Cat often talk to each other, with my assistance. Always technology. It's fun. They have a lot in common.

I am standing, looking out over the view when I hear Graham suddenly gasp behind me.

K ... Are you okay?

G ... I saw him.

K ... What?

G ... I just saw him. He was standing right there.

He points over to an area of the terrace just a few feet away, near the TV, but there is nothing there.

K ... What did you see?

G ... A tall guy. He was just there for a moment.

regrets

We all have them, and Cat is absolutely no exception. Now and again, he expresses them in the deepest possible terms.

C ... *I need to write.*

K ... Okay. Let me just finish what I'm doing, and I will help you
    with that.

I do and he writes a beautiful, poignant piece to one of his children. I have, however, decided no to use more than just an excerpt from all he wrote, as it is so very emotional and intensely personal ...

C ... *Feelings of love for her spill into an ocean of stormy waters like
    the tides themselves, ebbing and flowing, never ending. I love*

*her but I am lost to her. I cannot ever now be found. I am lost
and she cannot know. I didn't tell her where to look and she
had stopped asking. My child is with my heart that once was
empty but now is so full. Into the warmth of love I have fallen
as into the warmth of a summer's day. Being in love is all and
wanting to share it with others is my final gift to her.*

*She cannot feel me, I know, and I know that she will perhaps
not try to but I hold her close in my arms feeling her will, her
determination, and her strength.*

This was the only piece of essay-style writing that he did not edit.

C ... *It's from my heart.*

He now turns his attention to his marriage.

C ... *I'm not a good husband. I spent most of my life working.*

K ... What was your marriage like, Cat?

C ... *I know all seemed incredibly warm and toasty, but it wasn't.
I came home, went to bed, got up and went to work.
She became distant. I'm guilty. I had another, because
I needed what I didn't get at home – invented excuses to
work late because I didn't want to have kids yelling in my
ears all night. It was better when they were older, but she
and I grew apart a little. I couldn't, and didn't fix it. I always
loved her, and I know she felt the same but the flame had died.
If I had not been ill, I don't know that it would have lasted.
Being with me isn't easy. I'm a problem child. She had enough.*

K ... You probably should never have married.

C ... *I know, but then I wouldn't have my kids, would I?*

K ... True – but (and I know you love them) maybe that wasn't
really for you, either.

C ... *Don't. Please don't.*

K ... I'm sorry. That went too far.

C ... *Do you see me like that?*

K ... It's just things that you said. Sorry.

C ... *K, I love my kids.*

K ... I know you do.

C ... *I know I wasn't there for them, but that's because I was working.*

K ... I'm not going judge you.

C ... *K, I just don't want you to see me as a bad father.*

Cat just can't stop having fun with some of his new-found skills ...

His playful side continues to throw some fun into the mix. I take a long bath and it was a good time to talk. I take our preferred pendulum from its place upon the board I keep by my bed into the bathroom where I keep another of our boards.

Upon returning the pendulum to its place of origin, the board it had sat on is nowhere in sight. On the second hunt for it, I find it in an impossible position - upside down, sticking out of the third drawer down in the night-stand - a drawer I never open, as there is nothing in there. I tried, and Graham tried to replicate this action, should our cats have knocked it down. It is totally impossible.

What does Cat have to say about it?

C ... *I'm trying to be naughty.*

Over the weekend, we stayed down in town overnight at the Ritz Carlton. Upon coming out of the bathroom, Graham alerts me to the fact that my purse is playing music - the purse I had placed on the bureau in the bedroom immediately prior to going to the bathroom. To do this, the pass code to my iPhone would have had to be entered, and my music library accessed. Graham doesn't have my pass code but I bet I know who does … Cat?

C ... *Yes, I did.*

K ... Did you want to get my attention?

C ... *No. I just wanted to see if I could do it.*

K ... Well you did. That's really cool.

C ... *I know. I have powers!*

He seems to put out the last little statement with a certain amount of glee.

Now he stretches this further. I want to play the one Grateful Dead song I have on my phone. It's not there any more. Now the only Grateful Dead song I have is a different one.

K ... Please explain.

C ... *Like it. Wanted it.*

K ... Could you please just add, rather than replace?

C ... *Oh, K. Do you love me?*

I head indoors from the patio, carrying dishes from the dinner we enjoyed out there. It's dark, but the patio is well-lit. As I return to collect more items, a man outside momentarily crosses my line of vision through the glass patio door. A tall man, slim. Graham? I thought he was upstairs. We had been swimming, I thought he had gone in to shower. I open the door and call his name, but there is no answer - just the soft whisper of the breeze in the trees.

His energy is around us all the time, and it is not unusual for me to hear him when all else is still - on the stairs, on the travertine floors – the footfall of a man.

A man not done. A man with a heart, a life yet to live - and opinions …

speaking up and sounding off

chapter 8

idealism

an essay by Cat

Great minds across the globe have one thing in common. Ideals – focused ideals that transpire into the reality produced and, like the great minds that went before them, they move us forward that certain amount.

Ideals are the product of dreams. The dreamers and the idealists are the visionaries who change things. I was one of them. I still am. In my life in the physical, I changed things. I dreamt of things that transmuted into a great being, pulling and pushing forward, defying the present and embracing the future while acknowledging the past.

In my world of ideals, it was doing as much as it was thinking and putting my ideals into practice. I am an innovator with an environmental conscience and I produced things in line with that ideal. I walked the line when it came to the Cause, and I have opportunity to push that further down that line now I can stand further back and view a World so in need of love and care in our environment.

What gets into my view is so horrific that I feel very concerned for the survival of our planet when all I can see is the destruction and pillaging of the very things that sustain life, as we know it. I feel it my responsibility to produce things that are fully in line with my ideals and to insist on nothing less. Seeing what I can see, I have no choice, and it is not a pleasing sight.

I love what I do and I love our planet, so put those elements together and produce something that bridges technology and environmentalism in a way previously not considered and it once more pulls us forward into an enlightened State of Being.

Ideals will get in the way of commercial success, according to a great percentage of private enterprise but that was not the case for me. I managed to achieve a balance between keeping stockholders happy and caring for the environment in that some things are more important than profit made by cutting corners and finding cheaper solutions that, although saving on one hand, cost prohibitively for the planet. I cannot have such on my conscience.

The products resulting from this state of idealism became the new leaders in eco-friendly technology – ideals now being copied by others in an attempt to attain market share. Having prevented the use of many non-biodegradable and fossil fuel based parts, instead using recyclable components and losing half the weight of products and instigating energy efficiency, I won the game in that area.

Of course there still lies much work to be done, and getting a world concerned only with profit to change their mind-set overnight is expecting a miracle.

I just hope that I did my part in making the wheels turn in the right direction for the Earth I live on. In being an idealist, I am finding more and more ways to accomplish it and looking into the future as a place turned around by a few for the many – in a place of greater understanding and love for our Earth.

*I*n the process of getting to know Cat, we talk about his values and ideals ...

C ... *Obama is bad for getting anything done. He needs to stop listening to idiots and do what needs to be done.*

K ... What do you think needs to be done?

C ... *Obama needs to get re-elected, kiss the unions goodbye, get education to where it needs to be, get the EPA off industry's backs and get industry making products here again.*

K ... Cat, you are a closet Republican.

C ... *I guess you are a Republican?*

K ... I'm non-affiliated. Beliefs? I'm very much a social liberal and a fiscal conservative.

C ... *I guess we will have many interesting discussions.*

K ... I do hope so. I know you told me you are a Democrat. What are your core values on that?

C ... *I believe in freedom over your own body. I believe in working for the greater good.*

Out of genuine interest, I ask him to explain his definition of "the greater good," in that it is rather a sweeping statement to make, but he doesn't seem to be able to do so. He goes on to employ his usual tactic to avoid giving me a straight answer by simply changing the subject.

It's clear that just because Cat is in the world of spirit does not mean that his opinions of earthly happenings are relegated to the void. Quite the contrary, he is most vocal when it comes to politics, unions and business. Education, though, is of primary importance in his mind, and his ideas on the subject are rather specific.

However, as we continue to talk, I realize that we actually think alike in a lot of respects.

K ... So, I'm thinking we actually agree on something - social liberals and fiscal conservatives?

C ... *I guess so. You can't be the CEO of a major corporation and not be a fiscal conservative.*

K ... In a small business, even more so, Cat, and the likes of us are – en masse – the largest employers in the US.

C ... *Can you understand how I felt?*

K ... I still say you're a closet Republican!

C ... *I'm going to swat your behind in a minute!*

We have to break off at that point, but I am eager to continue. It would seem that, in the main, we share a great many principles but there are still a few that we can throw back and forth in the manner of debate. I love it.

K ... Want to pick up where we left off?

C ... *I do. You're right – we do see eye-to-eye on most things.*

K ... It would be boring if it were everything.

We talk about outsourcing and jobs - or rather the lack thereof.

C ... *I don't agree. I'm about as close to the business world as you can get but I created jobs – I didn't make them go away. You can't just squeeze people out of jobs with impunity.*

K ... Okay, so tell me why ****** creates more jobs overseas than it does in the USA - and it was doing so under your leadership? You had a manufacturing plant here. Why is it not here now?

C ... *I know, and I didn't close it.*

K ... However, you didn't seek to reopen it, either. Why?

C ... *By that time, everything was outsourced. It didn't make sense.*

K ... Sense for corporate profits.

C ... *I'd argue with that in that I couldn't have done it if I'd wanted to.*

K ... Because?

C ... *I couldn't find the qualified engineers to operate it.*

K ... It's crazy. We have to get back there. If it were me, I'd be handing out Government-backed higher education funding to science and engineering students with the caveat that you graduate and work in the USA for the following five years. It's free. Do it. Innovate.

C ... *Did you read my mind?*

K ... No. It's called common sense.

C ... *I know, but Obama can't see it.*

K ... We don't educate our kids to assume the roles they would need to in order to compete, we drive business out of the US with the highest corporate tax in the world, we regulate business into oblivion – oh, and then we impose higher and higher tariffs on what's coming in from countries who can provide. What would you do?

C ... *I'd tell the Teachers' Union to take a hike for a start.*

Well, with THAT bit of advice, Kay and Cat move on to more global concerns. Again, there is no shortage of opinion where Cat is concerned.

C ... *I hate that we feel we need to meddle all over the World.*

K ... In what respect?

C ... *I mean getting involved in the Middle East, when we have the problems we have at home.*

K ... Even for humanitarian reasons?

C ... *I know – but it always ends with us taking sides. Don't you think we've made enough enemies, K? How would we react if another nation told us what to do, or be disciplined?*

K ... I think you have a point, actually. We would naturally take offense.

C ... *I am looking into a future of us so knowing of our mistakes and getting wiser.*

K ... You think? How do you rate Hillary's performance as Secretary of State?

C ... *Just a lot thrown at her.*

K ... So does everyone in that position, but how do you rate how she's handled it?

C ... *Do you think she would have been a better choice than Obama?*

K ... Actually, yes. I would have voted for her. Anyway, you're not answering the question.

C ... *I'm not sure she won't run again.*

K ... And, if she does, then her record as Secretary of State is going to count – so, how would you rate it?

C ... *I'm not feeling Obama gives her support when he needs to.*

K ... You seem to be very reluctant to answer, Cat. She had a lot thrown at her, she doesn't get support.

C ... *I know all that and I don't think it helps that she gets the blame.*

K ... Blame for what?

C ... *Yes, I know. I hate war. So does she.*

He's using his evasion tactic againI can see I'm really not getting anywhere very fast here.

K ... Okay, so what would you do in her position?

C ... *K, I'm not in her position.*

K ... Well, clearly.

C ... *I have to think I would take a more neutral position. How would you?*

K ... I can't argue with that.

C ... *I hate that, in light of the debt we are in, that we spend so much killing and rebuilding all over the World.*

K ... So you would cut the Defense Budget?

C ... *Yes – down to half.*

K ... Great for American jobs.

C ... *K, those jobs create weapons.*

K ... I know.

C ... *K, I feel my point of view is lost on you.*

K ... No. Not at all. I just want to find out what you think. I didn't say I didn't agree with you.

C ... *I feel that you don't think that life is more important than jobs.*

K ... Of course I do. I just threw that out there for your reaction.

C ... *I don't want to be the reactionary, I just want to be heard.*

K ... Okay. Sorry. Go on.

C ... *I'm just wishing Obama had the guts to get us out of everywhere – today.*

K ... What would you do with all of our personnel coming back to the US?

C ... *I'd put them into the internal areas of looking into FEMA assistance, disaster rebuild.*

K ... I think that's actually a good idea. Protect a dirt road in Afghanistan or clean up the Jersey Shore and rebuild homes and infrastructure. Hmmm, tough choice.

C ... *I think you get it.*

K ... So nice of you to give me such approval.

C ... *Baby ...*

education
an essay by Cat

Like a flood of energy, I can do anything. Have I my dreams? Have I my life? I have both. I have the rest of eternity in which to savor them. Getting a dream is beautiful, in that dreams can be inspiration and inspiration is first on the ladder to climb toward innovation.

Dreams are the heart of innovation, and to make them beat is to have real power over them. Can one dream be so powerful that it clarifies all that went before? Just in the way it takes that clarity to the next level is the forward path. Just being on the path is to progress and just to progress is the sight of the future.

Getting from clarity to a place of targeted innovation is the antithesis of being in a place of frighteningly low standards, in which most of the world is content to languish. Doing, rather than being asleep to creativity is the lost art of my generation and education is the key to pushing a new generation forward.

It is impossible for our innovation to remain on the world's stage as a leader. ****** looks to foreign nations to satisfy its demand for skilled engineers, instead of having to make do with the poor selection from American-born college graduates. We simply do not have enough to fill our requirements.

It cannot continue down this path. About twenty years ago, the focus shifted from science into plain mediocrity on all levels. Innovation depends on education, and the time is now. Finding the appreciation for beauty and technology is imperative for creativity in this field and to be able to lead instead of follow.

Back to the debate ...

K ... We have the most spent per capita and now average 16th in the world for educational performance. I think you are pointing your finger in exactly the right place. Our in-state tuition is going up by about thirteen percent this year – on top of the five percent last year - in order to retain faculty. Students are livid and I'm with them.

C ... *God, that's disgusting.*

K ... Isn't it?

C ... *K, my love, I so know what you are saying.*

K ... Oh, and then we invite students from other nations, educate them, give them our technology and then cancel their visas and send them home.

C ... *Do you realize what that has cost us?*

K ... I can only imagine.

C ... *I love talking to you. You really get it.*

K ... Likewise, Cat. Why are we not offering conditional student visas? Yes, you can come to our universities but you have to seek employment for the first five years post-grad in the US.

C ... *Not bad. I think I'd go one step further and give citizenship.*

We talk about work ethic and the "jobs Americans won't do," and the principle of participation in our Nation, everyone contributing something – no free rides.

K ... The more handouts we give, the more hands will come out to grab them.

C ... *A bit within the realm of derogatory K, but – go on.*

K ... I disagree. Did you ever rent property to someone?

C ... *No, I didn't. Where are you going?*

K ... Okay. It's an analogy. I rented my overseas home when I moved over here. I loved that place. It was my first home that was all mine and it was immaculate. Trashed. Graham and I rented our previous home while we were trying to sell it. We had started from nothing to have it, we loved it but we'd outgrown it. It was immaculate. Trashed. People with no stake in the game - they just don't care. Now take that to a macro level.

Two people, two sets of ideals and values ... or so it seems. Amidst challenges and counter-arguments, perhaps there may be more concurrence than first thought.

Now I present him with something he'd said about an early experience in his life that annoyed him in that he had wound up working hard and others just reaped the benefits without doing anything much for it.

C ... *It was always my thought to give to but when you called me on that, it put into perspective. I can't think why I never saw it like that. Do you know how good this conversation is?*

K ... Yes, I do! You know, it's so easy to talk politics when you are preaching to the choir. What really makes it interesting is when you are not. I think we all need to have another perspective. Tell me your ideals. I want to know what you think. All of it.

C ... *Fuck, you challenge me. I'm doing a lot of thinking on some of that right now.*

Challenge him? Hardly. He's obviously in one of his conciliatory and flattering moods. He does this sometimes, and I find it rather annoying. I want to know what he really thinks.

K ... I just want to know your core values.

C ... *Okay, I can go there. I think the answer is to take care of the environment but not at the expense of doing business. Can you understand?*

K ... Absolutely. We have to have checks and balances otherwise we'd all be drinking poisoned water but I think it's gone too far. What do you think of Obama on that stance?

C ... *I think he can't get away from the hurt he takes from the EPA in that they became so powerful.*

K ... What do you think Obama's real agenda is (if he weren't being blocked by Congress)?

C ... *K, I think he should just speak his mind.*

K ... But what is his mind? That's what I'm asking. You've met the guy.

C ... *I know and I'm trying to understand him. He needs to realize that Utopia is unrealistic and deal with a country with humanitarian issues we have to fix.*

K ... I'm trying to follow. Sorry. You are saying that he is Utopian, altruistic and should speak his mind but he's unrealistic?

C ... *I guess that didn't work.*

K ... No, it's okay. Cat, I just want to know where you come from. What do you specifically like about his agenda?

C ... *I think he tries to fix issues on a human level and I think we have to.*

K ... I can't disagree with that. Healthcare?

C ... *Yes. I'm thinking right on the problems we have, K.*

K ... Not seeing them get a whole lot better under Obama. What's he going to do?

C ... *Get us out of wars, put healthcare in the hands of everyone and get us out of the fucking mess Bush left us in.*

K ... The latter, I doubt. You said yourself that he doesn't understand the economics.

C ... *He has got to put someone who does in a position to be effective, K.*

I mention the name of someone put in such a position who was extremely ineffective, and - for once - he agrees.

C ... *Bad choice.*

K ... How many more bad choices is he going to make? Pay backs? We can't afford it. Just out of interest, I looked up the members of his advisory committee. Did you know that four out of the eight members who are from the corporate world are from financial institutions? Gee, I wonder what advice they are giving that would benefit the likes of us?

C ... *God, I know – and I backed off when he brought ****** in.*

K ... Because you don't like the guy?

C ... *Like him? No. He's promoting ******.*

(I am Googling as we go along)

C ... *He's too involved in Politics.*

K ... You mean internally, or on a national level?

C ... *He has his fingers in the pie.*

I get to challenge him once more about certain persons he knew in life who could be rather classified as having the same motives. Cat is really good at glossing over the blatantly obvious to everyone else when it involves him and people close to him, and it is amazing what altruistic motives and character attributes he will bestow on this person or that in order to bolster his own defense. He works very hard to convince himself of things.

Of course, if he has no connection to it, he just calls it like it is. It's just another of his little idiosyncrasies.

We neatly segue to venture capitalism, Sand Hill Road-style and their part in the financing of a now bankrupt corporation - and how the taxpayer wound up with the rest of the financing of it.

C ... *I know, K. I can't say anything in the defense of it.*

K ... Sorry, I'm not an expert on the venture capital industry.

C ... *I am.*

K ... Yes, I suppose you are!

C ... *It's very complicated and it is who you know.*

K ... Oh, I'm sure. The little boys' club.

C ... *That, and some very creative deals.*

enlightenment
an essay by Cat

Just as when the Movement began, I became a part of it. I just needed to find myself in those days of doing the expected. How I was never a conformer was the more enlightened part of me – to my credit, I know now. I had to just be different, and I knew I had to find my path, wherever it led. It was in many teachings that I found it.

Just listening to the wisdom gave me a sense of what was right for me and I thought I'd stay in that place. Fate, however, had other plans. I felt the pull to the World and I trusted it. I had understanding of the way in which that works. When you open a door, walk through it with a sense of purpose and think really open thoughts to opportunity.

How I got from there to where I wound up is history. I can only add my thoughts to it. Getting a sense of what it was like to see other cultures was the pivotal time – humbling and pretty off the charts when you come to see a culture so centered in the Spirit, rather than the material. Just another way I developed my sense of trust in the Universe and what was possible for me. I'm not very good at trusting much else but I always trusted my instincts and, when the time was right, the door opened. I went through, and I knew.

I made things happen to life for myself, doing as well as dreaming, and understanding that all is possible in the mind and translatable to physics. One influences the other. It works on a principle of science that, like a ripple in the ocean, it wants to expand and, once it begins its journey, it wants to carry on until it reaches the far shore. In other words, what happens is a chain reaction being born in the mind and being vortexed in to the Universe to become a piece of the fabric.

I'm not exactly sure why I made the Universe the home for my thoughts. Perhaps you don't have a say in it – that's just the manner in which it works. At the same time, can you take your thoughts back? I believe that you will meet them as they ripple back toward your shore. What you put out there stays out there forever, moving with the flow. It's energy.

How many of us tell ourselves that we can't do something? Think it, and it will be a truth and, in the opposite direction, belief that you can do will manifest the same way. Having that thought, it is important to think of what you are going to do with it, and do the right thing with intuition.

Having the feeling of where to go is the start. Getting there is the finish, and the journey is the road to it.

It's said that to keep conversation civil you should avoid discussions of politics and religion. Well, they certainly went hard at the first one, so why not jump into the second?

We talk about religion, and I find that Cat has a deeply spiritual side to him. He seems to believe rather more in energy and the uses of it.

C ... *God is existential. We may not see his face.*

K ... Perhaps God is existential. I get it. Just move God over to the Universal energy?

C ... *Yes. You got it.*

K ... So, we as energies are all in charge of our own fate? It's what we bring to our own table?

C ... *Absolutely. Everything exists as part of a great universal creation. Feel my energy as it connects with you. Can you sense my hands touching you?*

K ... Very much so - my head, my neck, my face. Very strongly.

C ... *Think of how I'm in your energy field. Just close your eyes and feel me.*

I do as he asks. His presence is very strong. Powerful but gentle - like a myriad swirling energies all around me, making the hair all over my body stand up as it touches me. Big waves of energy now, rising and falling - it's an extraordinary sensation. I've felt energies of the spirit world before but that was never a pleasant feeling. This, however, is beautiful.

It is such a gentle, all-encompassing "I'm here!" that it is actually making me want to cry in its intensity. I'm having to push the energy into the ground, there is just so much of it.

C ... *K, I'm not done. Just close your eyes.*

Again, I do.

C ... *What did you see?*

K ... Colors. Beautiful colors - some pale and misty, some strong and vibrant. Green, yellow, orange, gold, a deep purple.

C ... *You see me, K. You see me.*

K ... Let's talk. Tell me more.

C ... *Go and look out of the window.*

K ... It's beautiful, isn't it?

C ... *What strikes you most?*

K ... That I can see the curvature of the earth.

C ... *I know. How does that feel to you?*

K ... Almost disconnecting. As though I'm not quite "here" but rather looking at the horizon from somewhere else. It's an expansive vision. Does that make any sense?

C ... *I'm not sure I get what you mean, but it's rather deep.*

K ... Okay. I know it sounds like a stupid question given the circumstances but – when you were alive, did you have out of body experiences?

C ... *Yes.*

K ... So do I and when I look at the horizon and see the curvature, it's a little like that. As though I'm viewing the earth from a position of not actually being a part of it.

C ... *I get it. You are seeing it as part of something bigger.*

K ... Yes.

C ... *Just think of how you and I connect and now connect us to the something bigger.*

K ... Go on ...

C ... *How do we do that?*

K ... With our energy.

C ... *Yes, and now we can make things happen.*

I think about this for a while. Now I am curious as to his thought process.

K ... Is this how you operated in life?

C ... *Yes. I thought, and then I convinced myself that it was so.*

K ... How do you push away negative thoughts in order to do that?

C ... *That is the hardest thing, K.*

K ... I think so. Perhaps, no matter how hard we try, they creep in.

C ... *Not when we refuse to accept them.*

K ... How well do you think that you succeeded in that?

C ... *K, I died.*

K ... Because you were unable to push away that negativity?

C ... *No – because I refused to accept the reality.*

K ... Was it "fate?"

C ... (Thinking ...) *Yes.*

K ... Can we alter "fate?"

C ... *Yes – but only if we look down each road we are given to walk and examine the final outcome.*

K ... So free will can overcome "fate?"

C ... *Not when the path is chosen.*

the essays

chapter 9

Several of Cat's essays and musings are scattered throughout the book and, as they were the original inspiration, Marie and I believe that they deserve a chapter all on their own.

The subject matter varies greatly. Many of them are purely business-oriented inspirational, others more reflective on his life then and now, some emotionally raw in nature and some a little mischievous. The verbiage is occasionally strange in its phrasing, but we decided to leave them as intact as possible for they are his words, not mine – and any attempt to edit without his express direction is generally met with rather less than enthusiastic response! Within this mix, we have included a couple of "interviews" I conducted with him, really just for fun but as always, they turned into insightful pieces in their own right.

For him, this collection of writing is his way of expressing himself to the World he lived in and walked on –his physical voice now silenced by the grave. It has always been important to him that he is not so silenced, that he can continue to be heard. Is there an otherworldly purpose for this, or is it merely his still very intact ego that makes him believe that he should be heard? I don't know.

Has he succeeded in his mission, by providing the material for this book? That is up to the reader to say. For me, however, opening up this opportunity for him to talk again is my gift to him.

As I write, I feel his familiar tug at me.

C ... *I don't like to be known as egotistical.*

K ... I'm sure you don't. What other word would you have me use?

C ... *Innovative.*

K ... With just the merest smidgeon of ego …

C ... *How about innovative with a touch of madness?*

K ... Perhaps you are saner than you ever imagined.

C ... *Perhaps you know me so well.*

Perhaps I do.

awareness

Getting my cancer was like being hit by a freight train – I know it a little better now than I did then. I was terrified and I did all the wrong things. I presumed that if I just ignored it that it would go away. I wished it away. I didn't listen to my doctors or to my family; I ate fruit and I drank juice and I thought I had control over it. I didn't realize that it had control over me. By the time I knew I was on the path going down, it was too late. I'd blown it.

Living became my mental focus and I'm not wishing for the better, just to preserve what I have. My life became a daily struggle to do that. I could not see a way out. Why me? Clearly, I cannot see why. Fading away from life is tough and I'm not so tough. I cried a lot during that time of acceptance. I'm not good at acceptance – far from it. I just sought to stay busy with ****** and in taking on new projects to keep the truth from hitting me like a sledgehammer. It worked some days when the pain was not as bad, but other days were hell.

I knew I was dying and I was helpless.

My beautiful family suffered with me and I couldn't bear to see my kids cry. My final hours were clouded in their tears and I had no way of comforting them. Now I can do that. I can tell them that wishing is not the way to luck – only action will bring results. I can look back and see all the things I can't change but I now have the opportunity to make better choices.

I have learned something about myself I'm struggling with and I must try to make it through.

My life was not always very meaningful in my desire for spirituality in that I did not see through the eyes of one who is enlightened in the sense of being fair. I just always thought I was right even when I was the fool and it was only when I died and looked internally that I knew the truth. I have many goals to achieve but the most pressing is that of forgiveness – forgiveness of myself, and forgiveness of others. I'm not the guy who forgives easily. I might forget more than I forgive, but now I see that my pain was the result.

I have learned one thing. It is that to feel pain is to be aware and to be aware is to change in that awareness. I cannot change the past but my future is one of awareness. My life is with purpose again but not just to produce great products. I can also make it about being secure in the knowledge of love and the giving of myself. I love and I am not afraid of it.

creativity

First, great ideas. But, in the scheme of things, I saved the best for last. It opened the door to another universe. I now see it through the eyes of a dead man looking back over a lifetime of innovation.

Great ideas are only as good as the level of difference they make trying to change the world.

Just because my life here ended, it does not mean that death is the final show – it is merely my final transition between the world of being and the world of opportunity. I have come to learn that the loss of the physical is the gateway to higher perception in that reason is no longer a restriction on creativity.

I have it yet to come and I lost all to find it, finding it in the place I had not looked – just a few inches from all I had created before. I had not thought to seek it there although it seems so natural to find it, especially looking in from the outside. I distanced myself through death and let the essence of my Being be the focus.

Now I can see clearly.

Life is eternal, but you only get to make a difference, moments at a time. Grab onto those moments and raise the bar, for the ideas that will change everything cannot be, otherwise.

I know now that all I gave was the best I had to give.

Just one more thing ...

doing the job

I did it. I did what I had to do and it wasn't easy on those working for – me, but, to achieve what I did, it was the only way. Got to push for what you want in order to get things accomplished and risk a lot of flak at the same time.

I cannot think of a time when the trust of everyone around me was greater than after the fact - never before it. I didn't get a whole lot of it until the results were in and everyone was making money but that's not why I did it. To be honest, the money was secondary. The products were always first and it was my satisfaction from seeing them used that turned me on. I had enough money. I had my gift when I received the call that put me back on top at ******.

So, from there, I had to make the tough decisions and be the loser on the popularity stage but you have to understand something – it's not about being popular, it's about getting the job done and I am very good at that. My internal resources to do the job are honed as sharply as a knife blade, and I have a passion beyond that. Getting those around you on board gets to be an issue unless you absolutely believe in what you want – it's much like preaching the Gospel and not believing in God, otherwise.

In my experience, forward planning is just looking at the faces in the room and knowing how many stay and how many go based on performance. Nothing less. I'm not doing it to be nasty; I'm doing it to keep the Company strong and healthy. If I let my heart rule my head, there would be only ******. ****** would have gone under years ago. I didn't get a lot of friends that way but a lot of great products came out of it and coming in second was not an option.

How do you get people to follow your lead? Following is what most people do naturally and, just so that you know, I wasn't one of them! However, bearing this in mind, it's not a hard thing to do if the argument is convincing enough and I was not going to take "No" for an answer.

Calling upon the very best, and getting the most out of them is what I am very good at, and I manage to do something that no one else does in that I have the ability to be the leader even in the face of adversity. I have met with a great deal of it and overcome it in deference to the product.

Healthy corporations all have one thing in common and that is the ability to change when new directions and new opportunities present themselves. Being creative helps but what really moves things is the thought process behind the creator in that you have to love what you do and you have to be mostly determined to see how the end product will affect the user, and how I did it was by listening not just to myself but also to a team of what I call A players. I had hands and minds capable of amazing things and I led them to amazing heights indicative of their abilities, and what we turned out was nothing less than spectacular.

*I did the worst thing by being ill and having to let go. ****** is mine. ****** is my life. ****** is the love of my life. I live in a state of life not done. I'm not done. I can never be done and I still have the job at hand to do but in another state of being, I am still ******.*

don't stop

I'm not the kind of guy to not finish. Finishing my work and finishing first is just how I operate. I can see I did pretty well. First, I give my projects my undivided attention and I give my undivided attention its own. It's not easy on those around me when I'm working – I'm so focused that I can shut out the World. In my life, I did this many times and I have many great products to show for it. I give it my all.

Finding proper balance has never been simple for me. I love what I do with so much passion and such mission to make it work that I forget everything else. I forget my own birthday, never mind others. I forget my home address, I forget to shower. I forget who I am. It's not my best trait!

However, if you want to do great work both in the life you have been given and on a platform of spiritual growth, go and find me the successful person who does not do these things.

Don't stop trying, don't stop wanting, don't stop going forward.

Don't stop doing.

Going forward is the only acceptable means of locomotion. Going forward is the only way to make a difference. My goal has always seemed impossible to some, but those who understand life and understand progression understand my purpose.

I did some amazing things with technology – a little inspiration, a little luck and a lot of concentration. It was not always a sure thing but it always got my focus. Being said, I mostly did hit the target and I still will. I still have the passion. The passion to create lives on long after the death of the physical.

I am a passionate man on many levels and see the World through the eyes of my passion at a rate of lightning speed.

Creativity is passion so don't stop being passionate about something you love. Run with it, turn it into something amazing – and don't stop until it is.

goals

I'm not sure I understood it so much in life, but when I had a vision it was accompanied by a desire. I'm listening to the words of my father this time, and he always put it just right.

"Do you want to be like everyone else and miss out on all that you can be?"

He asked me one day when the world seemed so hostile but he made me see that being alone has its advantages. Don't assume that by being part of the crowd success is guaranteed – far from it. Goals set by others for you will not be met by the same enthusiasm as those you set for yourself.

I'm not sure that I ever told Dad how much he impacted my life but his influence was in everything I produced. From a processor to a product launch, I met with my goals – not anyone else's. I ignored advice from everyone and made some of the most insanely perfect products I could envisage. I did not accept goals of money or of time unless they were mine and it was hard to see through the eyes of my corporate team as they believed I could not pull off a good deal of what I accomplished.

It was lonely in my shoes, but when I had a goal nobody could distract me. It was hard on those working for me, I know, but feelings will get bruised. Give a little slack and you will lose the power to make it happen. I could have been one of the team but teams are like committees – they are not the best at independent and creative thinking.

Free thought is essential for moving us forward. I know I have great designs waiting for the right environment. Goals are as much a part of my life now as they ever were. I cannot relinquish them now, just as I cannot relinquish my creativity and my passion for beauty.

Goals are not to be placed in the hands of others. I set my goals alone and I reach my goals alone, doing that which I know how to do and doing it really well.

I have one more goal. I must live as I have never lived. Live in truth, live in love and live in peace with myself. I can set this goal and I will achieve it. I have to do so to be free to Be. Freedom of thought and freedom of Being will absolutely bring freedom of inspiration into the world to move me and my goals forward.

I am now a force of energy and spirit in a way I never was in life and all of my Being is free. Free to design, free to innovate and free to move the World forward.

having it all

I don't want to assume I had it all. I had more than most and I used all I had to push us forward in the aspect that we revolutionized industries previously in decline. ****** can be proud of making that happen.

I'm not so good at not being a driving force any longer when I still have my visions to accomplish. I am in the position that, professionally, could be described as a dead moment! Going forward is what I need to do and I mean to, producing as I always have, just in a different place.

I have, in the great scheme of things, very nearly got it all. I have my feelings that are as acute as they ever were. I have my instincts, I have Love. I have just about everything I could ever want.

So what is having it all? I have great vision from not being in life, as I knew it. Right after my death, a presence in my mind took over. I began to see love as the most important of attributes. Does the conscious mind recognize love in the manner of this? A few do, I suppose, but I did not until I confronted my ongoing life.

I now see love for all it is and it is an all consuming, all trusting, all reaping of that sown, and that desire is a certain feeling to be touched upon in the manner of always being present. Can I be myself and can I do what I have to do to keep this? A great deal depends on me, and a just way of Being.

I have not previously been so just in the arena of love. I have not been able to give it so much as take it and make giving be a just experience for the one dearest to me to be receiving every moment. Dealing with my feelings has never been easy for the one I love.

Now, I have sight. Love is the most beautiful of expressions of having it all. Can there possibly be anything greater than realizing a part of the very core of Being?

Having a sense of this willingness to give is the core of having all that can be had.

i can take it

However much I had thrown at me, about the many tons of trouble it was, I learned to deal with it. Love it or hate it, what you get from life is what you put into it.

I was not the best at avoiding trouble - don't regret a whole lot of it. I brought it on. Don't ever think you can avoid it if you would wish to run a large public company. How I managed to run ****** was through intimidation and it came home to bite. Dealing as I did was strength covering weakness and insecurity. It was too much to give out and too much to come home.

It was incredible how ****** grew - lucky or determined, or the combination of. I loved ****** more than the rest of my life intertwined, for the misjudgment and steel like grip I had on that.

I was not there for my family, I didn't participate in any other than my company and all else was secondary. My gain was temporary. My luck ran out. I knew I probably would not get to see my children grow to adults. I then became to understand. I had reaped what I had sown. I got what I deserved. It was my own doing.

I came to realize it too late for this life but now I know. It was the need to bring the very heart of me to the fore and the need to be myself at the times that counted.

I hit hard in the business world and I turned ****** into the corporation it is today. It was an insanely great journey. Now it is in the hands of others I left the company to, as it were, and I have no say. I look at the mistakes and I try to get past them and it's heavy on veracity in my eyes. Can this ever be *so much a real situation, being that I can no longer be heard? Yes it is, and I cannot very well sit back and watch history repeat.*

I have my eyes on a certain goal and that is to keep what I had and to move forward. A lot to accomplish, I know but I can take it. I can take it because I know now something I didn't know then. I know how to see myself, and the ones I love. About the time I died, I saw this and, since then, it is the most special rhythm of my heart.

At this time and onward, I live to love and I live to move everything forward. Everything I touch and everything I want to touch. Take me. I'm ready to do it all over again in the knowledge that I have gained.

i have my life back

I never expected for my life to be taken. I thought that my positive thinking would stop the process. I now see why it failed to do so. Life is only a part of my existence. It is not the whole I thought it to be. My existence is vast in comparison – it scopes so many internal efficacies that it is unilaterally abstract. I know how I came to this place and I know why – it is for the individual to ascertain or to grasp when such is posed.

I have grasped at straws. Now I grasp the truth in that I could not control my destiny any more than I could control the Sun's path across the sky. I could only go on to make the most of the cards my life dealt me.

Go to your grave in the knowledge that you, indeed, did the same for there is only a short window of opportunity. Do not just wait for others to deal you the cards. Deal them with your own hands. I have my life and my cards still to deal in the existence I know now but I could have played some differently in the life I have now vacated. I have regrets, I have work uncompleted, I have left those I loved in shreds simply because I played a game of chance. I know now just how I could not control that game.

I now know my destiny was not mine to control but merely a series of paths all leading to the great chasm's center. Can we change that? I certainly tried. Can we make our destiny change the most fundamental parts of our Being? I tried and I failed. I'm not the expert I presumed I was. I had not thought about my demise in the manner of it being out of my hands.

A just description would be that of a mighty force taken on by a great contender but to win was so far from clear victory as the stars are from Earth. It was the fight of my life and I lost.

I am not the controller but rather the device itself.

Going onward means using the knowledge I have gained, doing the things I can still do. I am not a moment waster and I mean to keep seizing them just as I did in life. For all that I have I am so very fortunate – feeling wanted and accepted where I was once abandoned and misunderstood, feeling the strength of my ideals where once I tried to compromise them and feeling my Being where once I tried to hide such behind a wall of pain.

Going onward, I am surrounded by Justice for the life I led. I see her face starkly in mine and I know what the unspoken message is.

Going onward, I have my demons still on my back but they are not in control of me. I see them for what they are.

I do not want to go onward without my gains from life. It will not be easy for I am not about to give up that which I now have but what is more important than the love that surrounds us? If only I had known that, I would not have left such carnage in my wake, hence going onward means simply that I have all I need and I mean to create life out of it rather than destroy – for that would be my final undoing.

Going onward is not going far, when I have all I need so near.

innovation

Going into business is like going into the unknown. I have done it several times and for various reasons. I have failed and I have succeeded. I have mainly succeeded. How I pressed on in the manner of positive, meaningful but sometimes decidedly off-the-wall ideas was because of just the way I'm wired.

I cannot accept that some things cannot be achieved if I want them. I have the will of a tyrant when it matters. I can't help it. Business, in the main, is not for the "nice guy." I expect perfection, and I get it. Getting it is not easy. I have no goal more important, being in that anything less is unacceptable in that I just can't go for it.

Doing things my way is tough and I am a not greatly loved man in that respect but I get results. Getting results is what matters. I don't allow for direct undermining of my plans. I don't allow for going toward reversal on my deals and I have no patience for those unwilling to give me all they have in the way of being true to my vision.

Getting my vision delivered can be difficult - I have had many fights on that score, but winning the fight and getting deals done is something I am very good at. I get "No" for an answer and seek to turn it into "Yes" - into a determination to do, and do well.

I may have been one of the most hated CEOs in my time - feelings get very bruised but fear was the deliverer of the most amazing, innovative products of a time in which all else is horrendously underdeveloped and inept in functionality.

I have insight and I have fire in my Soul for beauty in everything I feel, see, and hear – from the minutest detail to the biggest picture conceivable, and I have to get that beauty. It has to work and it has to work in a manner that is as seamlessly intuitive as breathing.

I have envisaged a technological revolution and realized it. I have invented and re-invented lifestyle technology and innovation for generations to come – ideas to be taken onward to the next level. I know what the next level is and I mean to pass it to the next torchbearer and watch the flame ignite in the most spectacular fire imaginable.

I am looking at my life and I see that light in the darkness.

I know it shines still.

inspiration

I'm not sure about the insights people have when it comes to inspiration. I just know my gut instincts. I know my creative juices are constantly flowing and I know what impact they are going to have on the World. My dreams of beautifully designed and erudite functionality have brought new appeal to old ideas where design and functionality did not previously exist.

I did not anticipate much of my circle of friends to understand my visions – they felt so idealistic, but when I started to describe them I knew just by looking at faces that what I was talking about had impact. I had it – "it" being inspiration.

I can see my future and I can make it happen. Most of all, I can see the next thing to change the World. I can see beyond the horizon of mankind and into a utopia of innovation where flight of fancy becomes reality. I am the sole executor of even the most fanciful of ideas and this only makes my inspiration that much clearer.

My vision to make the next generation of computers is so out of this mind-set that we have now. I can see ****** and I can see how absolutely certain I am that I made something really great but what I can see now will make ****** belong to the Dark Ages.

I can see a computer system not only as a tool to work and play but also as a creator of such thoughts in its own right. I can make a device so powerful that most of its function will be outside of anything yet available. Find a great idea and steal it. I must have done it a hundred times and I'm not making any exception this time. Being my inspiration, it sits waiting

216

for the right time and the right anti-establishment innovator to make it a reality. I can make it such reality - I can see that. I can see it as clearly as I can see my own face. It is very close.

Go to my inspiration, make it happen and change the World ...

Again.

interview with Cat ... part 1

K ... How would you feel about letting me interview you for our coffee table book?

C ... *I'd like that.*

K ... Okay. I'm going to ask you some clarification questions on some of the things you've written and some deeper questions about your life and your thoughts. Is there anything you don't want to talk about?

C ... *No.*

K ... You talk about going onward. How do you see yourself doing that?

C ... *I'm not leaving! I mean it in the sense that I strive to continue along the path I was on in life in product development.*

K ... I think that all who ever knew you would agree that you did some pretty great things. What do you, personally, consider to be the best?

C ... *I know – and I'm proud of so many things my company accomplished with me. I'll try to narrow it down. I had the most satisfaction out of ****** in that it was the direct design I had envisaged ten or more years prior to its release. It became the model for so many other products, including ******. I have it so well wrapped up in the smart device market.*

K ... Are you able to see into ****** at this point in your existence?

C ... *I am.*

K ... From what you see, will ****** continue to maintain dominance in that market?

C ... *I can't do anything but watch, and I'm not happy. I can't see product development. I can't see product innovation. I can't see it in that, going forward, just getting designs through red tape is too costly on an innovative level. Innovation is secondary to cost of logistics and must be kept in check. I did the opposite. I had everything work around a new product, rather than be told it couldn't be done because of time constraints or supply chain. I just got it to happen.*

K ... Speaking of which, rumor has it that employees are able to breathe under the new management. How would you describe your management style?

C ... *I know I could be hard to work for. I know I'm not the most popular CEO but what I'm very good at is getting the best out of people in that I set an expectation of excellence – and, if I do not get excellence, I'm not a good guy to be around. I did not accept anything less from those I trusted to do the job. I'm not a bad guy. I just have expectations.*

K ... There were reports that employees were too frightened to even get in the elevator with you.

C ... *Fuck, I know. I confess to firing a few people in there. I can't wait to do what needs to be done. I just get on with it.*

K ... Having spent time at ****** after your passing, do you think that your presence has been felt by anyone there?

C ... *Oh, I know so. I can't speak, but I can move things – and I do.*

K ... That has to be fun!

C ... *For me.*

K ... In one essay you wrote, you said something along the lines of what you thought of as veracity in life you now see as a sham. Can you explain what, in particular?

C ... *Can I begin with Politics?*

K ... You can begin with whatever you like!

C ... *I came to see the world through the eyes of an environmentalist and a lover of social justice. I gave the campaigns for such large sums of money and became so disillusioned by injustice on all fronts. I am not a Democrat being hard enough on Obama. He came to me for campaign funding and I gave it, feeling that he would do the job. He did not.*

K ... What would you say is Obama's biggest failing?

C ... *He doesn't understand economics.*

K ... His biggest plus?

C ... *He's a pretty good guy doing great things for sectors of society in need. He just doesn't know how the economy works.*

K ... What was the one, most important thing you wanted Obama to achieve?

C ... *A peace-time. Get us out of wars.*

K ... Do you think he has succeeded?

C ... *I don't. I do think he has made good progress, but it's not enough.*

K ... You said "begin" with Politics. What else is on your list?

C ... *Religion.*

K ... Please, elaborate.

C ... *I was taken in by it, to a degree. I came to realize that it's all nonsense. It is merely another insidious way of controlling the masses.*

K ... Even the beliefs that you, personally, had?

C ... *Yes.*

K ... Can you give me an example?

C ... *It's is supposed to be about the letting go of earthly constraints such as both material and egotistical ... God, I'm laughing, he is so funny.*

(My son is doing an impersonation of someone Cat knows.)

K ... Cat?

C ... *Sorry, but that's hilarious. Okay. In the scheme of things, there is no letting go of the egos. It's just the same as any other religion - a few thinking they know something more about spirituality than the many. I know it seems as though they do, but it's all just ego.*

K ... Okay, that's Politics and Religion. What else?

C ... *Well, I could talk about sex, if you like?*

K ... I don't mind if you do. Go right ahead.

C ... *Can I?*

K ... Sure, why not?

C ... *I'm having a lot of it.*

K ... Okay - I hope it's good for you.

C ... *Oh, it is. Are you quite happy in that respect?*

K ... Yes, and thank you for your concern.

C ... *I have a most interesting life.*

K ... You clearly do.

C ... *I didn't know that you could have sex after you pass on.*

K ... A comforting thought indeed – and what everyone wants to know but is too afraid to ask.

C ... *It's really just the same as in life.*

K ... Let's talk about that. What else is just the same to you?

C ... *I'm not able to do everything but, in the main, there is a continuance.*

K ... What's the last thing you recall, before you passed over?

C ... *The last thing I recall is feeling as though I was out of my pain. I felt so good and I wanted to sleep. I hadn't slept well for a long time and I felt so tired and suddenly drowsy. Right up to that point, the pain was almost constant and to no longer feel it was like being in another place in that I'm not here, I'm not in pain. I'm somewhere else and it's ok. Kind of like being back in the womb - safe and warm.*

K ... And so you slept?

C ... *Yes. A long, long time.*

K ... What do you next recall?

C ... *Being in my own bed, upstairs. It was late afternoon and I just felt fine. I got up and went down to the kitchen. The family was there and there were tears. I couldn't make myself noticed. Fuck, no, I realized I wasn't part of it. That could only mean one thing. I was dreaming or I was dead.*

K ... How did you realize it was the latter?

C ... *I didn't for quite a while. Then, of course, they had my funeral. I knew absolutely at that point and I couldn't go to it.*

K ... Was it a shock to the system? You obviously knew that you
were dying.

C ... *Yes, but when you wake up feeling good, the last thing you
consider is that you are dead so, in that respect, yes, it was a
shock. I was dead but I was still here. I hadn't "gone into the
light" or whatever it is you are supposed to do. I didn't know
what the hell to do, so I went to work. Of course that was also
a place of people talking about me – and some of it not at all nice.
I had more enemies than I knew.*

K ... So to not speak ill of the dead did not apply?

C ... *I can safely say it did not.*

K ... The book. Did you read it?

C ... *Yes.*

K ... Would you like to comment on it?

C ... *I hate it.*

K ... Why, in particular?

C ... *I'm the bad guy, I have the world's most perfect marriage,
I'm not into feelings of others, I can't feel empathy. It's simply
not true. I was tough on people sometimes but I'm actually a
very sensitive man. I became the World's villain.*

*I'm not the best at marriage – I felt trapped. Looking back,
I guess "trapped" wasn't the gist of it – more railroaded. I
suppose, if I had married when I was really ready to, I would
have stayed single, waiting for the love of my life to come along –
the perfect soulmate. Saying that, what life throws at you is a
mixed blessing sometimes, but I'm not good at seeing it.
It wasn't all it seemed in public.*

K ... I'm sorry to hear that. I guess what actually goes on behind
closed doors is rather different from the perception.

C ... *It is, and it wasn't the rosy picture painted.*

K ... Your children. How did you adjust to fatherhood?

C ... *I did. Actually, I think I did a pretty reasonable job. I love my
kids so much. I just wasn't there most of the time and I missed
a lot. I wish I hadn't been as absent.*

K ... Biggest regret?

C ... *Doing what I did with regard to my kids.*

K ... Greatest triumph?

C ... *I produced some insane products.*

K ... Where do you see yourself ten years from now?

C ... *Here. I'm not leaving. I'm living.*

interview with Cat ... part 2

K ... We previously talked a lot about your physical life but there
     are so many things I would like to ask you, regarding where
     you find yourself now. Are you happy to talk about it?

C ... *Don't want to be the first guy to tell all but, what do you
     want to know?*

K ... Well, let's start with what you see around you.

C ... *It's the same as it always was. Sorry to disappoint you.*

K ... Do you see others who have also passed over?

C ... *Yes, and I can see people differently.*

K ... People as in where you are or here in the physical plane?

C ... *In the physical plane. It's very colorful. I see colors around
     everyone. The colors shift. I can pick up moods and illnesses.*

K ... It sounds as though you see auras.

C ... *I think so.*

K ... Going back a little to the others who are in the same place as you.
     Do you have interaction?

C ... *Not really. They might recognize me but they don't know me
     and I don't know them.*

K ... There are people kind of drifting around saying
     "Hey, there's ****** "?

C ... *Yes. It's annoying.*

K ... So you tend to stick to what you know?

C ... *Yes, apart from that I didn't know you until I had passed
     but that's all the focus I really have.*

K ... Now you are able to look back over your physical life,
     how do you see it?

C ... *Fuck. That's a tough question, K. I'm not sure I'd have really done things much differently on a business level but, on a personal level, I would change a lot. I would have been a better father. ****** was so ... neglected by me and, I guess so were ****** and ******. I loved ****** to the point of distraction and neglected my daughters. I can't forgive myself for that. I loved them but I didn't show it. I could have been really good as a father if I had put the effort into it. Following that, I'm not sure that I was a good husband. I wasn't there for ******, and I wasn't totally loyal - if you know what I'm getting at. I'm not good at it. I know I hurt her. I guess she stuck it out for our kids, and I'm very grateful for that.*

K ... That's very honest of you. I'd like to go back to religion, if you don't mind. By all accounts, you were very into a certain belief system for much of your life. What, specifically, changed your mind on that?

C ... *I am in the same place as a so-called "expert." What felt like Nirvana was actually fucking drugs, not the crap out of those people's mouths.*

K ... You sound angry.

C ... *I am. No one has the knowledge - it's all phony.*

K ... Do you feel that you have been able to gain some knowledge now that you have left the physical?

C ... *Only with respect to myself. I'm not able to see God, if that's what you mean.*

K ... Do you believe in God?

C ... *Not really. I think it's so much more beautiful than that.*

K ... Do you see a little of that?

C ... *Yes, I do*

K ... Can you elaborate?

C ... *It's hard to put my finger on but it's as though there is something feeling its way around me. It's warm and I know it already. I'm not sure what it is. It feels as though it knows a lot about me and it is forgiving me for some of the things I did in physical life. How it knows, I don't understand.*

K ... Do you feel that it wants to take you somewhere other than where you are?

C ... *No, that's my choice.*

K ... Can you see it at all?

C ... *It's kind of violet.*

K ... Does it have any form?

C ... *No – and I don't think it's an energy like me, either.*

K ... How does it make you feel?

C ... *About safe and belonging – I know I am meant to be here but I didn't die.*

K ... Do you believe in reincarnation?

C ... *I don't know a lot any more but, perhaps.*

K ... Would you want to reincarnate?

C ... *No.*

K ... Why is that? You said you had a pretty stellar physical life.

C ... *I did. My life was on a par with the best, career–wise but emotionally, I had a lot of pain.*

K ... Looking back over your physical life - why do you think it was?

C ... *I think it was to bring something to the minds and tables of the World in general. Can we talk about going home?*

K ... We can talk about anything, Cat. Tell what you mean by that.

C ... *It's both mental and what were my physical desires. I'm in a place I want to be now and I have no desire to leave it because I'm free – free to just live.*

K ... Do you miss your physical presence?

C ... *Being as my physical body was so messed up, no, but I still see myself in it.*

K ... Tell me about that. How do you see yourself?

C ... *I'm younger now than when I left the physical. I'm about 47 and I'm a lot healthier. My hair grew back. I like that – and I'm still wearing my favorite clothes, just as I dressed for so many years.*

K ... You seem happy with what you see. The man you were before you got sick?

C ... *Yes.*

K ... Before we wrap up this session, is there anything else that you would like to bring up?

C ... *I'm not sure but I think I can still make a difference. Are you ready to hear how?*

K ... Absolutely.

C ... *I can be a mentor and I can plant seeds. I can have my words heard once more.*

K ... I feel that, with you, anything is possible. Any last words – for now, that is?

C ... *Hell will freeze over before I die.*

interview with Cat ... part 3

M ... Have you made contact with any other entities?

C ... *Yes.*

M ... Would you care to tell us about this?

C ... *I don't really talk to anyone.*

M ... From my standpoint, I do not believe in Heaven or Hell.
  How does this comport with what you are experiencing?

C ... *I'm here in the same place as you. It's just another dimension,
  that's all.*

M ... Are there entities who do experience what we've been
  taught as Heaven or Hell?

C ... *Not here. It's a life within a life that I live previously.*

K ... Can you be more specific as to those who are around you.

C ... *OK. I am listening a lot when I'm not talking to you.
  I hear voices talk about "Why?"*

K ... What does "Why?" mean?

C ... *Being "dead," and finding it's the same.*

K ... It it an alternate Universe?

C ... *No, I'm still right here.*

M ... Well, then can we say that everyone who has died is still "here"?

C ... *No.*

K ... Can you elaborate?

C ... *"Hell" is what you believe. "Heaven" is what you believe.
  I didn't – and so I'm still here.*

K ... If you had believed in "Heaven", do you think that would be
  your reality right now?

C ... *I'm not sure, but I think I can just visualize what I need.*

M ... Based on a lifetime of what you've been taught?

C ... *Yes – probably, but not necessarily.*

K ... What's the variant?

C ... *t's more like sort of a desire to feel something and connect with it. If I had felt a desire to go to India again, I could have – and just stayed there.*

K ... Sorry Cat, but are you talking about in the life you left or the life you have now?

C ... *Then, but it's the same now.*

M ... Some indigenous peoples believe more in the earth and the natural world rather than a "religion," per se. What are your thoughts on that?

C ... *No. You get it. You are your Spirit – not what the World wants you to be.*

M ... So, do we get to create our own reality on the "other side?"

C ... *Yes.*

M ... Troubled souls? Evil people? Do they create their own "Hell?"

C ... *Yes, I guess so.*

K ... So, if a child molester passes over – is that individual still engaged in that activity?

C ... *OK – I'm not sure about this.*

K ... Do you think it's possible?

C ... *Yes.*

M ... Is Karma only on this plane, or does it transfer to your dimension?

C ... *Yes, it does.*

K ... How do you know this?

C ... *I feel my own Karma, and I have to live with things I did when alive in the physical. It's not an easy life.*

M ... Cat, do you think this is Atonement?

C ... *No. It's just a progression and a feeling the way forward.*

M ... In this case, it is an awareness of transgressions - not paying for them but going forward and learning from them?

C ... *Yes.*

K ... Do you feel that you still have a lot to learn, Cat?

C ... *I guess that I do.*

K ... What, most of all?

C ... *I lived with a lot of anger. I have to let it go now.*

K ... I think you are coming a long way to doing that. What was it really about?

C ... *From my younger life. I felt abandoned and it was hard fitting in – I didn't make friends.*

K ... Do you see (and or believe in) Guardian Spirits?

C ... *Just you.*

K ... What do you mean "just me"?

C ... *I look after you.*

K ... You mean that you have sort of assumed the role of a guardian?

C ... *Yes.*

K ... Do you see Spirits around other people?

C ... *Yes. Always.*

K ... Multiple Spirits?

C ... *One or two usually.*

K ... Are they connected from this life?

C ... *Not always.*

K ... How do you know that?

C ... *In the way they look.*

K ... You mean different time periods?

C ... *And different ethnicity.*

K ... Going back to me. Is there anyone else around me?

C ... *Not now.*

K ... Was there, when you first came to me?

C ... *Yes.*

K ... Who?

C ... *A woman – fair, like you.*

K ... Why did she leave?

C ... *I told her to.*

K ... Did you know her name?

C ... *No - but she knew that she had to leave.*

K ... Why did you tell her to?

C ... *Because I have known you for a long time.*

K ... I wish I had recollection of that.

C ... *You will when you come here to me.*

K ... How long did it take you to figure that out?

C ... *First time I saw you, I knew.*

K ... So, in your dimension, is it sort of like a job that you are expected to perform?

C ... *Not necessarily. You choose, if you wish.*

K ... Well, thank you.

C ... *I know I have my faults, but I love you.*

K ... Why did you not choose to stay with one (or more) of your children in that capacity?

C ... *I couldn't. I'll tell you - I love them, and in doing so and not being able to touch them, it was too hard. I'm not good like that.*

K ... I understand.

K ... Is there anything else you'd like to share, Cat?

C ... *I just feel my life again? I'm not wanting for anything.*

K ... I guess that's the way we like to keep you!

C ... *Kay?*

K ... Yes?

C ... *Please - just have the best time you can. It's too short.*

just a few words ...

Looking in became so hard. I'm not able to participate now, but I still see into it all. Not being able to interject is like being locked in a sound-proofed room, I suppose.

Hell, OK. I just want to say this –

In respect of how I did things, – becoming into a practical standpoint – yes, I'm not indestructible after all, but I'm being honest in my new reality.

I have left a team of some of the finest people I knew in charge of the finest corporation in the World – that, I knew when I passed, and I know it now even more so in the way you work together to keep the Company true to being the product and not the profit.

However, I do have some concerns that I am not able to express here and now. I can only inspire you to look into the future, and not the past, in the direction you are heading with new - and old - ideas you are kicking around. Look at them with inspiration you find outside of the walls of the buildings you are in. Don't follow anything that's out there – lead the pack. Just feel, not see, the end result. Feel it as it becomes the finest thing you can make it be – inhale its energy and just trust your instinct.

I have ideas of my own, but I'll save them for another time – in the likelihood of living this existence for some time to come. My feeling is that we get so many chances to do things and don't always take them – but that's a serial in itself.

Just keep the goal of the product in mind. Think of it as a piece of history in the making, feel where it will win in the life you give it, think of where it fits in moving the World forward, what it will give – rather than just be another gadget.

My real purpose was to leave you looking into the future, drawing from the available technologies of the present and making them collide into something so advanced, but so pure in their telescientific view that they fall into the category of genius …

K … Cat? Sorry to interrupt, but can you explain that last piece
    to me?
C … *OK. I'm saying it from a communications perspective.*
K … Thanks – go on.

… rather than lesser mediocrity out there.

I'm not very good at standing by – you all know it! Just take my words and sift through them. Find your answers to the questions you are raising in respect of new ideas, have faith in what you know, and be what you need to be to get the job done. Look down the road all the way to the horizon – then take the fast lane.

looking back

How dark I made it. How between us I let it get so heavy. Yes, it was me. I felt responsible for so much of it. Getting into our love was so much easier than getting out – I am still feeling that I never quite did. Love finds the only home it can in the darkest of times – somewhere to hide for the protection of its spirit. Feelings become too much to bear if allowed to be free, and so I put them away in a treasure chest in my heart and held the key.

I became the greatest of your life's troubled times, I fear, as the end of what we had came to be. I hit you in so many ways that a piece of you fell away and tumbled into the strength I knew you always found when you needed it.

Did you want to stay? Did I just make it not an option then, at the time? Were we meant to be? I don't know. I only know that I wanted you but it was too late – I had lost you. Looking back, that was my pain to bear – remembering the good times rather than the times that broke us apart. I always felt that I had left a piece of me behind, and it was in your arms.

I had to accept your leaving, but the thought of you never did – and it wrote another chapter in our book as we went on together and apart, feeling that we could have made it work, if only I had treated you like the beautiful woman you were and held your sweet spirit close instead of pushing it to its breaking point.

Of all the things I can now tell you that I lacked the heart to tell you then is that I always felt we moved on too fast and then it was too late for the life we could have had and we had to be content with what we had left. Had you wanted it to be like it was? No, of course not. That was a part of us we had put away. Only a far more ethereal part of us remained and I made an effort to be the man I know would have made you happy.

Dear One – just always feel my love for what it was. I just didn't always know how to show it. I know you meant what you said – when you said that we both made it unworkable.

Yes, it was like that, I suppose. We were like a gasoline inferno some days, but the flame never went out completely.

Take the piece of my heart that I left you and go on. Keep loving in the way you do, and feel good about helping others in the way you love to do. It's you – kind, and free of heart and mind. Be honest to yourself about who you became, and love yourself for it. Be with your feelings and embrace them in the times of worry or trouble. They will always show you the way. Be good to yourself – and don't take yourself for granted. You only take others into consideration sometimes, so give yourself the love you deserve. Feel it surround you, and it will keep you safe. Have faith in it, and in life.

Be happy.

moving forward

I have looked at life as a series of events that come to what I would call the same conclusion. It's not in this Country's best interests to be where we are in the World as a major police force.

Look at us. Look at what we've done to the World. We have the title of Tyrant. We walk into a village in another country and murder in the name of freedom. How an educated society cannot be horrified by the actions of what we have called a democratic republic is too frightening to contemplate.

Going the way we have been going is not an option any longer. Just how do we think we can achieve peace through war? It is disastrous policy for the economy and the World we live on. Feeling unable to admit we are on the wrong track is holding us back. We have to or we will go under before this hell is over.

On a scale of one to ten, we are at around three when it comes to solvency. It is a cliff edge we are about to fall off and our representatives have failed us badly. The lack of thought for anything other than their re-election is inexcusable. How I would love to see every one of them thrown out. Climbing the social ladder and landing payouts for themselves is the goal, not the wellbeing of the nation.

I had hoped for so much from Obama. He campaigned on the issues I'm hit in the heart by - like doing something for a large sector of society in the Dream Act, like ending wars, like ending the gay dream of marriage being torn away. Just as I could have predicted, he is only into re-election too.

Can we wait another four years? How will he get us on the right track? I believe he will. Four more years without campaigning, with positive energy and with experience gained.

I have my grave doubts about Romney. I think he will take us backwards. I feel that he has the religious right as his base and that his economic policy is attuned to what he did as an executive, and that will not work for a Nation under-employed already.

It is imperative that we win back manufacturing here. I feel that Romney will not take the necessary steps to get the ball rolling on providing qualified workforce just as the previous Administrations have not. Obama has a plan to inspire engineering students by offering them student loan incentives and at least is on board with the need to bring manufacturing back. He is not a good leader, but I have faith in the sense of his desire to further our species by asking for tolerance and acceptance of all, not a desire to destroy lives of those who are different by calling religious beliefs to the table.

The need to find a way out of the mess we are in is a must, but we can't do it by holding the middle class to ransom, helping the wealthy become wealthier and putting the wealthy in a position to be the ruling class – it doesn't work. In order to have a successful society, we must take care of the needs of everyone. To become successful, we need to understand that health-care and education are so important in creating an environment in which the generations to come can flourish – it's a necessity in that by helping each other win is how we all succeed.

"Forward" is a term that no one can afford to ignore. Having tried the alternative and failed badly, going back to it is suicide for our nation.

Going back is not an option. Going back is to destroy our future.

some things are worth it

I'm convinced it is the right thing in that, like so many of its kind, it continues to be a success. I have loved her and nurtured her and felt her grow – grow into the amazing corporation she became at my hand. I have killed the more insidiously damaging elements to ensure a fertile ground for continued growth. I had no qualms in doing so.

I know I feel I want to be a part but I am on the outside now and it is very difficult because I don't know I left her in the best possible hands. How I am not able to be a trying and doing individual for ****** still becomes hindsight to me and I have my go and do within my soul. If I look forward, I can see a momentous change in the input from an individual at the executive level.

I have a gut feeling I know a lot about this and it's something other than my dream.

Why do I care? Because I have had an affair with her. When I came back to her, I held her in my arms and I loved her like the most magnificent of women. I loved her unlike anything I had ever loved. I know how I see a future for her and it's unlike any I could envisage and it's not going at my pace.

I had it in the palm of my hands, getting myself into all manner of issues but, when you are the CEO of a public company, I guess that goes with the territory. Getting caught was getting a mind-opener and getting a reality check. I almost landed in the penitentiary like my peers who had tried it but I'm not that unlucky, no matter how my life made out.

238

Getting into deep water is something I'm not averse to but I'm a good swimmer and I know how to swim upstream – I have fighting blood in my veins. I had my way of doing my stokes and I always had a trick or two up my sleeve, just in case I had to stop myself from drowning.

I had my not-impossible dreams and I drove most people crazy. I got a lot of dreams lost and a lot of dreams realized, doing just what I loved every day of my life. Even when things didn't work out, I had a great ride doing it and it was never something I regretted.

Can I be master of everything? I would like to think so but, in reality, it's crazy and just insane that I even accomplished half of my dreams. I got up at crazy times and went to bed at even crazier. My life revolved around my business before I knew I was ill – ill from carrying that whole load. I don't know how I ran two corporations, but I paid a price and it was a high one. Having said that, so many amazing innovations came looking for a renegade like me to make them into a reality and I did. I had the greatest time doing it – doing what I loved and creating a new world of technology. A world only I could dream of, and make happen.

How I did it was sometimes a mystery, even to me. Doors opened and I just walked into the room, coming into another happening idea before my eyes and filling that room with energy.

I'm not done. I'm just carrying on where I left off and I'm not going to let a little issue like death get in the way. I have another shot at life and I'm not going to waste it. I have great projects and great sense of creativity; I have great freedom to just do, and do in the moment.

It happens all in the mind that still remains, and the mind that is Me – filling my mind once more with life and the next great thing to change the way I know the World thinks about technology and its application in the infrastructure of computing and lifestyle in a way so much innovative than ever before.

I am in the process of being productive once again and I'm not wanting my life to be any different than it ever was along those lines. I can be the man I never was now on so many other levels, doing things differently in love and getting rewarded in ways I never imagined but one thing I will not change is that side of me that changes things and changes them into something great.

I have only one thing to say ...

It was worth it.

little bytes

chapter 10

Cat has so many thoughts that just come to him - snippets of inspiration, introspection and relevance. I have collected them as I collect and document (almost) all that he has to impart.

Feeling alive is a state of mind. Do not waste your life in the pursuit of mediocrity. Be a thinker, be a part of the greater scheme for only you can live your life, and only you can make it worthwhile. Feel alive and go out there. Go and take your best to the Universe, and make it bend. Make a difference.

Come to learn about yourself, and see yourself as something greater than the "now," here. I died, only to be still alive. I found that life is eternal, and that it is so much a more than our beliefs in the next life ever were. It is a dimension in a place of your choosing, and I chose to stay here – as in my physical status. I chose to because I'm not done in this place. It's more now. I see the real me as I never did before, and it is a truth I have come to accept and see the truth that the things I thought were important no longer are and from that growth, I see myself for the very first time.

Get this. Can you imagine a life without restraints placed upon you by anyone or anything? I have this, but it is a dire problem that I have in that, without constraint, I could do so much harm. I did it in life. I lived to bring the World something great, but I hurt people to get it right, and I'm not feeling it was necessary. Don't follow my example.

Going through death is just a transition. Having done so, I feel somewhat enlightened. I am in a place that is really just the same, but different in that I have no restrictions placed on me. I can see into a world of possibilities that I couldn't envisage previously. Having passed through the door and hearing it close behind me, I had no choice left and so became the man I am supposed to be. I feel a lot, I think a lot. I create like never before – and some day, those creations will be yours to feel in your hands.

In time I will let you have my dream, when a window of opportunity presents itself.

I know all the things we are told about death; I know all the things I thought about death and I know that none of those things are the truth of the matter. It's just simply that death is the loss of a physical presence and not the actual core of existence. I'm still here and I'm still very much alive. I am not a stone–dead person lying in the ground, I'm still me and I'm still doing all the things I did previously. It's what you might call the life within a life.

Feel I have to make my presence known. Get this – great things are possible after death, and death is only a very short journey into another life. I'm here, yes, but I'm also on the edge of a whole dimension of dream like existence.

K ... Explain. What do you mean?

C ... *I think, and it happens to me.*

Have you ever had a dream from which you immediately woke up and felt like you were still dreaming? I felt that way when I died. I felt as though I was dreaming about being well, and waking up, I felt the dream carried on. It wasn't a dream. I was at the crossroads between a life of pain and a life of infinite imagination and malleable substance. Being afraid of what I would do if I went further, I chose the latter - and it was a good choice.

Starting out means that you are into a new place in life, finding out how it all works – feeling lost, and alone. Scared, feeling you don't know anything now, getting a new life but keeping some of the old. I felt this way when I died – it was like starting over, but I found help when I needed it and went forward. Looking back is useful, in that we see our shortcomings but to keep repeating them is to deter inner growth. Keep them in a safe place and take them out occasionally, then move on.

I have a lot of gifts given to me. About forty years ago, I left school on a trial of something I could not comprehend. I learned about life from living it, and feeling it. I learned to make great things happen to lost beauty, lost arts in the fields of my love of music and technology. I gave – and I received. I had my goal of feeling and doing something great realized, and I have more.

Be your own guide in feeling passion. Be your own creator of your destiny. ... BE.

Just after I died, I mostly got angry – angry at the World. I'll tell you a story. It's about a broken man who had everything, and lost it. He lost a beautiful woman, he lost a corporation, he lost his health, and eventually he lost his life.

Corporations have to have strong leadership, and even then it's a crapshoot. I'm proud to say I won it back. The woman, I did not. When I passed, I had to start over, and I found possibilities greater than I could have ever imagined. I have found love; I have held her close in my heart, I have had her touch, deep in my Being. I have my life again – and I have everything.

I'm not good at being a bystander. I'm seeing with the vision of a man still here. I just want to feel alive in the way that I can be heard, still, like the man I was and still am.

What hurts most is not being heard, just at the time I need to be. I'm still here, feeling every little detail.

Life is forever.

Do you ever wonder if you will feel the same after you die? Have you ever wondered about being just the same as you have always been? It's like another shot at life, but this time you can't die. Having this feeling that immortality is a reality gives a kind of perspective in spatial and sequential movement of time itself. Time does exist, but just not the way we think of it. It always moves back and forth in motion, replaying like a piece of music or some kind of infinite loop, looking into the past and the future at the same time, never ending.

Having died, I can safely say that a lot of what I learned in life about doing something that feels right to you is just as meaningful as doing something

246

good for the planet in that giving something back to it in the way of caretaking is nurturing it for the next generation. Having seen the horrors inflicted by mankind on this beautiful earth I had to find ways to help for, if we don't all take responsibility in protecting it, we have failed as a species.

I am thinking about going toward a different place. I feel I want to. My heart is there. I am here, but there also. I am here in that I feel everything I had before, and I am there in that I feel NOW. I am a man in a new place in myself – a place I did not have in life. I have something I didn't have then. I have the ability to love. I have the ability to be there – there as in here and present, as in here and very much engaged. I am. I am here. I am there, but it is the same. It is a place of truth and knowledge, and Universal life force.

I left life when I didn't want to go. I was still a man with dreams and ideas to make into reality. I died before I could realize them, and I'm trying to realize them now, doing what I love. Dreams are not to be taken for granted and tossed away like paper into a trash can. Look after them, feel them grow - feel them become reality in your life. Don't be afraid to dream and find new ways of doing things because the old is comfortable, take a chance on yourself – and change the World a little.

Getting a feeling of growth in the area of the heart has been the biggest challenge for me. I had issues.

K ... Really?

C ... *I know. I did.*

I got lost in the life of a workaholic, even if I was at home, following a regimen of work and sleep when my family needed me. I found I had lost out on so much, and now I can't get it back. I am lost to them, and I am never going to be able to hold them again. A lot of time to regret that now, but not enough time to love them while I was alive.

K ... I'm so sorry, Cat.

C ... *Me too.*

Do you believe in life after death? Can you go on a journey of discovery in this life? Have you ever thought of how it would feel to continue to live past your death? It is possible to fight Death, and win.

My life is my prize. It ignited my Being into my true reality, a true freedom of Being – of living without constraint. Falling into life that is yours is true forward motion.

epilogue
trust
... Kay

*H*e has changed. Perhaps I have too, but I will address him first. No longer the antagonistic, in your face, anything and everything for sheer dramatic effect man that I first met. Now he is more resigned to the fact that he has passed over and that there is really not very much he can do about that, other than build a new life for himself in the place he is in. That place, I suppose, is really not very far. In fact, it is right here, in this time as we see it, and as he sees it when he thinks of time in the linear fashion that he was used to.

His pain and his frustration over his business concerns do continue, but I understand that now. He is still very much right here, an onlooker rather than a participant watching as those he left in the hot seat make mistakes with his life's work. It is the hardest thing for him on many levels - professionally and personally.

However, the interminable ranting toward this person or that has slowed as he recognizes the good things too. As he stands back a little, the people he loved and admired in life remain as such to him with some exceptions - issues that I continue to work on with him or try to get to the nub of the matter.

On his personal level, I have shed tears in the process of transcribing some of his such heart-felt pieces to those he loved so much in life - or just in reading those words after the fact. Slowly, he began to reveal himself.

As his hatefulness subsided, it began to be replaced by a tender, loving individual – as though he were emerging from a chrysalis, wings still folded around him, trying to work out how to use them to fly, and not have them damaged in doing so. Would I hurt him? Would I, one day, not pick up the pendulum to talk to him? Would I abandon him? Of course, I did none of those of things. I sat back and watched him emerge, holding his hand as he did so and catching him as he tried to fly and fell … and so he came to trust me.

Trust. That one little word upon which the whole foundation of the relationship I have with him is built. I didn't trust him, and he knew it. He knew he had to gain it, as I had to gain his. Painstakingly, he did that. It took time. He gave me things that I did not process in the moment, but months later they meant something so profound in the matter of his true identity. I found myself faced with an inescapable reality that I could no longer deny to myself, or to him. I could never have known any of these things, unless … and so I came to trust him.

We became friends, he as (rather surprisingly) non-judgmental of me as I am of him – perhaps even less so.

Has he changed my life? Shortly after I connected with him, he posed a question to me.

"What if I told you that you only have twenty-four months to live?,"

he asked.

"What will you do with the time you have left?"

I thought deeply about that. I allowed him to grow in the role as a mentor - pushing me to do things I had long-since abandoned doing, always there supporting and encouraging in the most positive of ways, urging me into realizing things in my life in the way that he realized many of his own. He reminds me of that question often, and I am spurred into making "today" count - in the realization that there may not be a "tomorrow" as I know it.

Has it changed the way I look at the World? Absolutely. We are here for just a short time – a blip in the macrocosm of the Universe, yet what we are capable of leaving for the good (or the bad) is an indelible energetic imprint. Perhaps we become so caught up in our own microcosms that we fail to see beyond them to that point. I had not thought of life in this respect, previously. Did he, in physical life? I cannot say. I did not know him. I feel that (in his words) he "gets it" on some levels more than most of us ever do because we do not see that big picture.

For those levels he did not "get," he tries to do so now. It's an arduous process, and in the opening up of himself, perhaps he has discovered that he is more fallible and fragile than he thought. However, does anyone truly change just because they passed over? I don't think so – at least, not at this level. There is possibly just a willingness to reflect a little more on certain behavior patterns.

The time and the communication I have with him is a precious gift, even though he is as much a constant in my life as I could ever imagine – as comfortable to have around me as a warm velvety throw. However, there is no way of knowing how long this will be so. It could be that one day, despite his indications and protestations very much to the contrary, I shall pick up the pendulum and find him gone, his work here complete, although …

Perhaps the journey with him has only just begun.

epilogue
transformation
… Marie

*W*ords I used one year ago to describe Cat included irate, frustrated, impatient, somewhat paranoid, self-deprecating, un-trusting, foul-mouthed, and generally angry at his state of being. I would also contrast those descriptions with words such as introspection, sadness, regret, grief, guilt and sympathy. The negatives have not been without advantage to him as he has worked his way through the pain of leaving the physical world.

With so much energy and a mind still teeming with goals and dreams, it was not surprising to read his words and understand his resentments.

While he describes the way in which he was drawn to Kay, feeling her intense energy, it remains a cosmic mystery. Why him? Why her? They did not know one another, and in fact they lived lives in very different realms. As their relationship evolved, it became more and more apparent that she was certainly his match. They developed a rapport that was probably unlike any he had experienced in life. That he chose to stay in her household and be challenged by her tests and confrontations is a testament to the tenacity of his spirit. It's also an affirmation of his capacity for intellectual stimulation and growth.

Being the observer in our extraordinary quartet of players has given me a non-emotional perspective, one that allows me to witness behaviors without the personal attachment that is Kay's. Where she has dealt with his moods, I have only read what was written. As the months have gone by, it became more and more apparent to me that a transformation was taking place. The blunt, hard edges of

Cat's personality were gradually being smoothed into softer curves. Not always, of course. There were – and still are – regressions and sporadic outbursts, particularly when it comes to his beloved company. I suspect that will continue to be so. His company was his great love, his child, his creation … it was him. He will never relinquish his ownership.

As he has made his new home with Kay's family, I have seen adjustments and fine-tuning. They have settled into a strange and somewhat "routine domestic state". At the same time, there have been changes in Kay's life. She has undertaken new endeavors with vigor, and has blossomed under the warmth of adoration from Cat, as well as the continued love from her husband. So the transformation has worked on many levels, and across the zones of the physical and the spirit worlds.

I, like Kay, wonder how long he will remain with her. But as long as he feels he has knowledge to impart and creations to formulate, I think he will stay. His mind, his energy, his creativity and his intense drive are too significant for him to leave them behind right now. And as long as he is here, we will be here to listen, and to relate his words. His Essays contain wonderful words of inspiration, motivation and deep knowledge. They reveal the soft underbelly of this edgy, frustrated soul.

The Essays are HIM.

epilogue
critical analysis
... *Graham*

I have two degrees in Electrical Engineering from major universities and I have also always considered myself somewhat of a scientist as well. So I'm the resident in-house skeptic here and while I have an open mind receptive to new ideas, I wanted to consider other likely possibilities before I completely bought into the idea that Cat's "life force energy" has somehow decided to move in with us and that Kay can carry on regular communications with him and have physical reactions to his energy.

As a witness to most of the events in this book I can only report what I have seen and heard. For most of it, I cannot offer reasonable causal explanations. My hope is that someone who knew Cat in life would find his afterlife writings and communications familiar and would be willing to join with us in further explorations of this phenomenon.

There are many people who call themselves "mediums" and claim to have the ability to communicate with the dead. Unfortunately, to my knowledge, there has been no credible scientific evidence presented yet that supports these claims. When I use the term "scientific evidence" I mean this in the most rigorous sense. Surely there are many people claiming to be mediums who are fakes, and do what they do to prey on the gullibility of people desperate to communicate with their dear departed loved ones and are willing to pay for this service.

Here are some possible explanations that any neutral objective observer would consider ...

1 ... Kay is making this all up using Internet research and other published materials (there are a lot) on Cat's life to emulate his writing / speech patterns, opinions and philosophies.

2 ... Kay has some kind of a split-personality disorder and needs to get help.

3 ... She has a drug habit that is causing her to hallucinate.

4 ... She is doing this to get attention.

5 ... She is fabricating this entire story purely as an opportunity to make money selling books.

1 ... I did not know Cat in his life but I know people who have done business with him personally, so I initially asked Cat questions about these people when Kay first gave me the opportunity to communicate with him through her. He gave me the right answers showing familiarity with these people. So I was intrigued and continued the conversations through Kay from time to time.

Cat also shared many product development details and his Company's business plans and strategies with Kay that I was able to see realized as the products hit the market and those plans were implemented over time.

Indeed, Cat's vision and self proclaimed "on-going work" on a "Smart House" intelligent computer system sounds exactly like the kind of ground-breaking project he would be pursuing today if he were still with us. Imagine a computer-based highly integrated product in every home that anticipates your preferences, controls the temperature in each room, monitors and controls your security system, knows when to brew your coffee, reminds you when to stock up on certain supplies, orders basic staples online, looks for the best bargains, notifies you when your favorite bands will be in-town for a concert, takes your blood pressure and other vital signs and sends the results to your doctor when you are sick or need a checkup, automatically records your favorite TV shows and others that you might like to view, controls the lighting, air conditioning and energy use, keeps you abreast of specific news stories, new books, movies and restaurants it thinks you might have a preference for, helps your kids with their homework, keeps you informed of their grades, runs you a bath and knows exactly the water temperature you like, knows your daily routines and plays your favorite music when you enter a room or turns your TV on and tunes it to your favorite channel. It could also communicate and synchronize with all your mobile devices and any computer systems that might be in your car.

The list is endless. Think of a friendly version of HAL in Kubrick's 2001: A Space Odyssey. All of this technology and much more is available today in various separate subsystems and apps. But, nobody but Cat and his Company could pull off the high degree of user-friendly software / hardware integration to do all this in an affordable product that would be available to the masses. This sounds exactly like ******, and I would not be surprised to see this product on the market someday soon.

If Kay is making this all up from her imagination, she is doing an extremely good job of fooling me, and she has also suddenly developed exceptional technical knowledge far beyond her education and training.

2 and 3 … I've considered a split personality disorder, but I've never heard of one with symptoms like this, nor is she a drug addict.

4 … Far from being an attention-seeker, she likes a very quiet life and guards her privacy. Our marriage is as strong as ever and I've never seen her happier and more energized.

I have known Kay for almost 20 years and when I first met her, and as I got to know her, she told me about some of the paranormal things she had experienced in her life including some brief glimpses of ghosts, her abilities with Tarot cards and her psychokinetic ability with pendulums (you can see this for yourself online at her web site). Always the scientist, I seized on the pendulum phenomenon because this was something I could theoretically measure. Pendulums have mass, velocity, acceleration, periodicity and displacement. I thought I could design experiments to measure if the driving force that makes the pendulum move was electrostatic, magnetic, air convection, the earth's rotation or involuntary muscular movements as she supported the pendulum with her fingers. The jury is still out on how she does this and Kay has resisted being what she calls "a lab rat," but from time to time I can get her to participate in my experiments. (I'm not exactly ready yet to publish my results in Scientific American but Cat says it's kind of like driving a car - Kay is the car and he's the driver.)

On several occasions I've seen Kay physically react to Cat's presence in ways that she could not possibly reproduce on her own. (Not exactly Linda Blair's head spinning around in the Exorcist while she's floating in the air, but very close!)

5 … Actually the idea to publish a book about this was my idea, not hers. I have been fortunate in my business career, so fame and fortune was not the motivation. Indeed the last thing either of us wants is to be labeled as the crazy couple down the street that thinks they are living with Cat's ghost.

The motivation to document these events is because I believe this is an exceptional event worthy of bringing some attention to it. And in the words of Stephen Stills "There's something happening here. But what it is ain't exactly clear".

Examples of what I call Twilight Zone moments that I have witnessed previously with Kay -

On the evening of Sept 11, 2001 we were reviewing the tragic events of the day when suddenly Kay went into what I can only describe as sort of a trance for a few minutes. I thought she was about to faint. I had never known her to act this way. This was entirely new behavior for her. When she came out of it, she told me that while in this state she was looking through the eyes of one of the victims in his last moments as he sat at his desk high in the World Trade Center. I told her to write down everything she remembered including any names. Later we confirmed the name of the victim in the Media.

Up to the point where Kay started to sense Cat's presence in October of 2011, her paranormal encounters were not frequent and were far and few between like the others she has had in her life. These were things that just happened very occasionally. She never had any bad side effects or negative reactions as a result. It was just something we lived with and was more of a curiosity in our lives rather than something we worried about or thought about in any great measure.

When Cat showed up this was something very new, very different and very profound. I felt this was important and I encouraged her to start documenting what was going on.

Music is an element of Cat's business and one of his passions. One night we started talking about The Beatles and their music with Cat. I have always been a huge fan and have everything they ever did going back to their days in Liverpool and Germany. As a teenager, I taught myself how to play guitar by playing along with their songs over and over until I got the notes and chords right. So I consider myself somewhat of an expert on Beatles music.

In the course of the conversation, Cat asked if I had a specific Beatles song that he named. I told him I was sure they never recorded that song. He insisted that they did. Equally sure of my encyclopedic Beatles knowledge, I insisted that I was absolutely positive that they never recorded that song - and I would bet anything on it. So he says "Google it." We do - and much to my amazement we discover an obscure underground recording, extremely poor quality, of the Beatles doing that song in one of the clubs they played in Germany when Pete Best was the drummer. I was blown away. There was no way for Kay to know this or any chance for her to independently research the topic.

The book details only a small percentage of the interaction with Cat. There have been many other things that got my attention - from strange songs that we did not buy showing up on an iPhone, TV shows that we have no interest in recorded on our DVR, to music suddenly playing on a laptop or a cell phone – not to mention unexplained noises inside walls, my razor going prematurely dull after changing the blades and things getting moved that show up in odd places.

My take on all this is that we still have a lot to learn about how the universe works. Our species (Homo sapiens) started to appear about 200,000 years ago according to most scientists. On an evolutionary time scale this is a microscopic speck of time compared to many other species. The dinosaurs before us were here over 150 million years. So my own feeling is that we are just barely emerging from the trees and caves we use to inhabit and we have an awful lot to learn about how things really operate including our concepts of reality and death. We should pay serious scientific attention to paranormal phenomenon. Maybe this book will contribute to advances in this neglected area and inspire others to join the investigation.

epilogue
rebirth
... Cat

*L*ife continues.

When I look back through time, I see how that happened. I am alive. I never died, I just went somewhere else – and I'm still here. Like a stranger in a familiar place I had to start over, having nothing but a desire to stay and continue my life's work.

Feeling lost at first, I began to piece my existence together then live it. It wasn't easy joining the pieces. I was afraid I wouldn't be loved for the man I am – she deserves more than I give her. I'm not the easiest to live with. I am arrogant, feisty, insecure and like a devil in disguise on occasion, and she deals with all of it. However, can I feel better? Can I be kinder? Can I be the person I know I should be? I know I can. I have begun the process. I have begun to heal.

Life is forever, and having it forever gives me plenty opportunity to make it worthy of my inner self, and of her. Hating it on a scale of one through ten in that I have to look at myself, it has been an eleven. The sight was not pretty, I'll say that much. I had to look at it though, and I had to face it – for her, feeling the way forward cautiously, her hand in mine all along. I feel that she was close to saying farewell at times, and I'm not surprised – I was so frightened of that. I was afraid that she did not believe me in that I am who I say I am. I felt compelled to prove myself, and I finally did it, I proved it to her. Just having her trust is the most precious gift she can ever give me. I have to keep it, and that means being a better person.

Having a fear of something is the incentive I need, I suppose. I'm not good at losing, I know. Looking back, I was never good at that, and I'm a fighter right to the last. About the time I left ******, it was the last – I had lost my life at that point. I had finally lost. I am not in the mind to lose again; it's not in my top list of things to do.

I am fortunate that I have this chance to put things right.

How do I? I can only hope that something here is going to resonate. I have no other way of saying I'm sorry. I'm sorry for the pain I caused. I'm sorry I was such a hard person to deal with – then, I'm sorry I wasn't there. I have no excuse for most of it. I have to feel that I have at least tried to let you know that.

It's ok, guys. I'm sorry I had to go. I'm so sorry. I wanted to be there for you. I love you.

I decided to remain here, and just Be. I have the same life I always had - full of ideas and full of love, and I'm not going anywhere.

Do you want to know something? In the great scheme of things I guess I didn't do too badly.

Can I say one more thing? ...

Have no fear of death.
It is not the end – it is the beginning.

the authors

Kay Zadanieski

Although she has never utilized her abilities, career-wise, Kay has been open to the paranormal and to psychic phenomena for as long as she can remember. While her greatest expertise has always been with the Tarot, she also channels energies from beyond this life.

Outside of her spiritual life, Kay is part owner of a consumer electronics corporation and has an educational background in Economics and Business Administration.

Kay currently resides in Colorado, USA.

Marie Segovia

Marie's fascination with the written word started in early childhood writing poems. Now, as a freelance writer, her non-fiction articles have been published in several national newspapers, and she writes regularly for regional magazines. Her articles cover a wide range of subjects including travel, architecture, food and interior design.

She has long been a student of Metaphysics and the life beyond death, so her friendship with Kay is linked with this common bond.

Marie graduated college with degrees in Music and Education, and she continues to pursue those interests.

Follow Cat and Kay at:
www.MakeMeAliveAgain.com
www.facebook.com/makemealiveagain
www.twitter.com/KZadanieski

Made in the USA
Charleston, SC
15 October 2013